MIND OF THE ATHLETE®
Clearer Mind, *Better* Performance™

Dr. Jarrod Spencer
Sports Psychologist

"It's increasingly important for athletes and coaches to recognize that training the mind is as critical to athletic success as training the body. This book is the premier tool for making sports psychology accessible to athletes."

Lindsay Gottlieb, Head Women's Basketball Coach, UC Berkeley,
Berkeley, CA

"This book is not good…it's great! Dr. Spencer helped me to connect with my players on a deeper level. I am forever grateful to him for it."

Dominic Jose, Research and Development Liaison, Los Angeles Dodgers,
Los Angeles, CA

"Dr. Spencer's book will help you win as an athlete and beyond your competitive years. This book is a must read."

Matthew Myers, Co-Founder of GiANT Partners,
Edmond, OK

"Every athletic office should have this book as a resource. *Mind of the Athlete* offers valuable insight into how the mind affects performance. It provides an in depth understanding of the daily struggles athletes and their families experience."

Robert Hopek, Retired Athletic Director,
Hall of Fame National Interscholastic Athletic Administrators Association,
Easton, PA

"Any athlete who wants to take their game to the next level should seriously consider the mental concepts in this book. Dr. Jarrod Spencer will improve your performance."

Amy Swensen, 2x USA Olympic Field Hockey Goalie,
Norfolk, VA

"*Mind of the Athlete* is a strategic read that demystifies the mind-body-spirit connection. Dr. Spencer offers non-jargon-laden prescriptions for five maladies worth confronting. Athletes will deepen their joy and faith, as well as develop their performance on the field and in life."

Rev. Dr. Alf Halvorson, Senior Pastor, Memorial Drive Presbyterian Church,
Houston, TX

"I can say with 100% conviction that learning how the mind works will provide you with a competitive advantage. This book explains it best!"

Kevin Cassese, Head Men's Lacrosse Coach, Lehigh University,
Bethlehem, PA

"Every parent raising a child involved in sports must read this book. It provides practical coping skills to develop an athlete's emotional health for performing at higher levels."

Jennifer Saks, mother of youth athletes,
Bainbridge Island, WA

"Sport coaching should include the 'total' athlete: body, mind and spirit. Dr. Spencer's book exudes wisdom as it explains the mind in a way that every athlete can understand and apply."

Dr. Jeff Duke, Author of 3 Dimensional Coach,
Orlando, FL

"This book provides important insight for any athlete to overcome psychological roadblocks and gain a mental edge. I am a firm believer in Dr. Spencer and his mantra: *Clearer Mind, Better Performance.*"

Todd Beckerman, Head Wrestling Coach, Brown University,
Providence, RI

"As a basketball player and coach in both the US and Ireland, I've experienced firsthand the power of the *Mind of the Athlete* concepts. Athletes in our Sport Dream Academy love them. You will too!"

Dr. Paul Cummins, former Division 1 & Irish national team basketball player,
Dublin, Ireland

"The single greatest factor that interferes with performance is a lousy state of mind. This book teaches athletes how to clear away negative thoughts and let their true potential shine through."

John O'Sullivan, Author of Changing the Game Project, former Pro Soccer Player,
Bend, OR

"There is not enough time placed on understanding the mental side of competition. Mind of the Athlete gives athletes a foundational resource to not only understand how their minds work in all areas of competition, it provides skills to create a clearer mind for better performance. These principles are something that my daughter and I continue to reference on a regular basis, as she progresses through her collegiate soccer career."

Hardie Jackson, VP of Sports Marketing and Partnerships, EvoShield, LLC,
Bogart, GA

"Dr. Jarrod Spencer has done a great job explaining the processes of the mind and the complex issues we all deal with. Through the answers to our "why" questions, the narration of true stories, and the examples of realistic solutions, this book is useful for both athletes and coaches in understanding how to reach maximum potential."

Kristyne Cole Russell, former 2x Captain of University of Michigan Swimming,
Ann Arbor, MI

DEDICATION

For John.
You taught me the most about clearing the mind.
I am forever grateful.

TABLE OF CONTENTS

ACKNOWLEDGMENTS

Above all else, I want to thank God for giving me this opportunity to share the messages He has placed on my heart.

To the men and women who so selflessly give their time, talent, and treasure to serve others in sports—On behalf of all the people you've impacted, I say a sincere thank you.

To the community of Phillipsburg, New Jersey—Sports play an integral part of our lives here. Thank you for teaching me, and us all, valuable life lessons that transcend athletics.

To my Little League coach, Dan Beers—Thank you for encouraging me to be a scholar athlete by showing me the wonder and excitement of a book, *The Hobbit*.

To Dr. Glenn Asquith—Your spiritual guidance has made this book happen. Thank you.

To Michelle Trifiletti & Alyssa Lombardo—I deeply appreciate your assistance with this book.

To the people of Fellowship of Christian Athletes, Athletes in Action, and Upward Sports—Keep ministering to the sports world. Your impact reaches far beyond what we can see.

To the Mind of the Athlete staff—Our mission and ministry thrive because of you. Thank you.

FOREWORD

BY MATT MILLEN
4x SUPER BOWL CHAMPION

Not everybody loves sports, and not everybody loves competition, but there is competition in everything. Whether it is school, your work, a sport, a pick-up basketball game, or hopscotch, you name it, there is that element of competition in everything.

As you climb up the competition ladder from backyard games to Little League to high school, college, and professional sports, competition increases. Your willingness and your desire to know and understand how to compete becomes more intense.

Understanding all that goes into competing is really what is driving this book. The easiest way to understand how competition works is through athletics because you can measure it. There is a winner and a loser.

Understand that there are a lot of ways to prepare for a competition. Most of the time, we think of it in the physical realm because that is what we know how to do. I can get bigger, faster, stronger. I can study my opponent. I can look at all these different things and then physically be ready for what they are going to do. What gets overlooked, for the most part, is the mental aspect of training, which is far more important than the physical part.

Clearly, you have to have physical skills to be able to compete in certain sports. In every sport, and in every competition, there is a level of athleticism that is required.

Once you have demonstrated that you can physically compete in an arena, the difference between winning and losing lies within the six inches between your ears. It is what makes you different, what sets you apart, what allows you to be able to compete consistently at a high level.

Understanding how the mind works relative to competition is the beginning of reaching your full potential.

It has been said that 90% of sports is mental. I disagree. I think it is 99%. Once you possess a certain physical skill level, your mind carries you through. I have seen mentally strong, less physcially gifted athletes defeat and dominate more skilled but less mentally prepared athletes. You hear the familiar refrain, "How did that guy lose?" The difference is not the size or the development of the body, male or female, it is the development of the mind.

That is why competition relative to the mind interests me; I can't get a read on your mind until I compete with you. I don't know what you are until we compete. That's what makes it so much fun. You can get clues to your opponent's mindset by studying him. But to really know that opponent in that instance on that day, you have to compete with his or her mindset. To me, that is the essence of sport. That is what makes competition so much fun.

Why did David beat Goliath? Why do underdogs win? There are a lot of reasons. One of them, buried in every underdog victory, is the clearer, more focused mind.

When I was initially exposed to elite competition, I had to learn and understand how I worked before I could ever figure out how somebody else worked. That was in college at Penn State University. It probably took me two years to figure it out. I was a starter all four years, and by the end of my sophomore year I had learned to control my anxious feelings before a game, my butterflies, my heart pounding out of my chest, and I learned to focus on who I was playing, and what I needed to do to win. That was the difference between winning and losing. My junior year I started to be able to really focus and thus I became an All-American.

By the time we had won our second Super Bowl with the Oakland Raiders, I understood how my mind worked. I understood how to prepare my mind. I understood how to prepare for individual opponents. I understood how to win.

By the time I got to my third year in the NFL, that's when the game mentally started to slow down for me. At that level, it's who's going to adapt and adjust fastest. I played a long time because I was able to do that. Certainly, there were players who were more gifted than I was physically, but no one could out-prepare me mentally. I found a way to win. Period. That all started from the neck up.

It has been said that the beginning of wisdom is knowledge and the beginning of knowledge is awareness. Become more aware, and become a better player by learning how your mind works.

This book teaches you how to understand yourself and your opponents. It teaches you how to process your emotions, such as fear and anxiety. All are driven from the mind.

I believe that a clearer mind leads to a better performance and a focused mind leads to one's best performance. The only way to focus is to be clear. If you can clear out everything else and focus on what has to be done to win the competition, you will be better at winning.

Dr. Jarrod Spencer defines in this book how the mind works. While some of it may sound unfamiliar, when you get to the end of the book you'll have a better understanding of not only how the mind works, but how you can work your mind.

INTRODUCTION

"Learn to control your emotions,
or they will control you."

—Edgar Martínez, former Major League Baseball player
and current hitting coach for the Seattle Mariners

Clearer mind, better performance. You've experienced it in sports and in life. The trouble is that too often, you can't seem to stop your mind from racing—so many thoughts and feelings. You feel overextended and overwhelmed. Your life has become overscheduled with constant pressure to perform. You feel tired. Emotionally drained. Your competitive drive is waning. And your performance is compromised. You are looking for a way through this dilemma. You feel stuck.

You are not alone. We are seeing alarming rates of mental-health concerns among young people, including athletes. In fact, NCAA Chief Medical Officer, Dr. Brian Hainline, declared mental health the No. 1 health and safety concern in the NCAA.[1] Too often, athletes are taught to hide their feelings of doubt, depression, anxiety, and fear—they can be viewed as a sign of weakness. However, real strength is being able to work through these emotions in a positive and proactive way.

Sports are emotional. Yet athletes today are struggling emotionally more than ever. This is a recipe for disaster. It is also a great opportunity. You can begin down the path of sports psychology and learn so much about the mind. As you understand the mind, you will be amazed at what you can do and how much better you can do it.

Athletes are lagging behind in being equipped with the psychological skills necessary to manage the emotionality associated with the pressure-cooker world of competition. Sure, "suck it up" is a good technique, but if that is your primary way to cope with stress, it is grossly insufficient. There is so much more you can do to regulate your emotions. You can learn how the mind actually works, and then you can stop fighting against it and start working with it. You can learn insights and skills that can help you thrive under pressure. You can unlock your potential and start competing at a level you know is inside of you.

As you walk this path, it will become even more evident to you that many of the people on your team may need this information, too. You may wish to share with them that you've found a way through it.

The incidence of mental and emotional health problems among young athletes is troubling. Consider these statistics:

- Almost one-third (31.3%) of all college students experienced difficulty functioning due to depression, and more than half (51%) stated that they felt overwhelming anxiety in the previous year, according to the 2013 National College Health Assessment.[2]

- 2 years later the 2015 National College Health Assessment[3] revealed 35.3% of students experienced difficulty functioning due to depression and 57.7% stated that they felt overwhelming anxiety in the previous year. That's a 4% rise in depression and over a 7% rise in anxiety in the two years from 2013. This is trending in an alarming direction.

- Loneliness is a common factor related to difficulties

in relationships. Among student-athletes who reported relationship problems in a recent Sport Science Institute study, 85% reported feeling very lonely in the previous twelve months. The data indicate that loneliness is highly correlated with both anxiety and depression.[4]

- An American College Health Association survey found that, on average, most student-athletes report four nights of insufficient sleep per week.[5]

The growing concern for the emotional health of our young adults was captured well on the cover of the September 2014 issue of the American Psychological Association's magazine *Monitor on Psychology*. The caption reads, "College students mounting stress," and the photo shows a female college student in a state of anxiety as she is holding her phone in one hand and her lowered head in the other hand, while grimacing in angst. The article contains a compelling graph (see below) showing that anxiety levels among college students are literally heading off the chart.

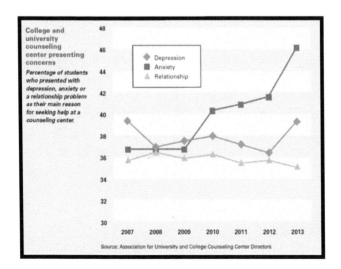

College and university counseling center presenting concerns

Percentage of students who presented with depression, anxiety or a relationship problem as their main reason for seeking help at a counseling center.

◆ Depression
■ Anxiety
▲ Relationship

Source: Association for University and College Counseling Center Directors

Taking care of your mental health by pursuing the help of a professional is admirable. Unfortunately, athletes (and others) who seek professional help for emotional or mental issues are often seen as weak and inferior. The good news is that the sports world's view of this stereotype is slowly starting to change. It is my hope that this book is another catalyst for this change. It is my prayer that people may read this information and find validation and encouragement for their valiant mental battle that occurs silently and privately inside of them.

Sports psychology is the new frontier in high performance. While athletes know a lot about building muscles and balancing nutrients, few know how to handle the emotional side of sports. Too many athletes fail to reach their full potential due to this underdeveloped area. Those who recognize the importance of achieving mental and emotional health, in addition to physical health, are performing at higher levels than they ever thought possible. You can, too.

It is often said that sports are 90% mental. If that is true, then has anyone ever taught you, as an athlete, how the mind actually works best? This book does just that. It explains to you a simple yet profound model of the mind. Once athletes know how their minds work, it is amazing how they can have their minds work easier for them, not against them. It is my hope that this book will provide you with deeper psychological insight and broader self awareness, which will lead to better judgment and a realization of your full potential. Many athletes have benefited from this wisdom and I hope that you will too.

This book contains three parts:

1. Part 1, "*Clearer* Mind, *Better* Performance," describes the main parts of the mind and tells how each helps you store memories and process information. A key point this chapter makes is that the preconscious mind, one of the three parts of your subconscious mind, is often clouded with unprocessed thoughts, concerns, and other material. You cannot perform at your optimum level until you learn how to clear your mind.

2. Part 2, "Clearing the Hurdles," describes five hurdles, or obstacles, you face when you try to function—in sports, academics, or life in general—with a clouded, flooded preconscious mind. Strategies for overcoming these hurdles are also provided.

3. Part 3, "Relief from the Flood," provides you with five practical, effective strategies for processing the thoughts that flood your mind constantly—even at night, when you're trying to sleep—so that you can perform at a higher level.

At the end of each part is a list of key points to remember.

Let's get started! The sooner you learn how to clear your mind, the sooner you can achieve better performance.

PART 1:
CLEARER MIND,
BETTER PERFORMANCE

"Make sure your worst enemy
doesn't live between your own two ears."

—Laird Hamilton, professional surfer

Muhammad Ali knew the power of the mind. He stated, "The fight is won or lost far away from witnesses—behind the lines, in the gym, and out there on the road, long before I dance under those lights." The fight was won or lost first in his mind.

Sharon Wood, the first female from North America ever to reach the summit of Mount Everest, said, "It's not the mountains we have to conquer, nor the elements, but rather it is the self-imposed barriers—those limitations in our minds."

Tennis legend Venus Williams professed, "In the sports arena, I would say there is nothing like training and preparation. You have to train your mind as much as your body."

You know that the mind is as vital to your success as your athletic ability. Yet it is likely that until now, you've done little to develop the mental side of your game. You've probably invested a lot of time, money, and energy in travel teams, tournaments across the country, elite camps, and the very best athletic gear. But have you ever read a sports psychology book? Have you ever watched a movie that contains sports psychology themes? Have you ever listened to a podcast on sports psychology? Too often, the answer to these questions is no.

> **Has anyone ever taught you how the mind actually works? Probably not.**

Has anyone ever taught you how the mind actually works? Probably not. That is the purpose of this book. I will teach you how the mind of an athlete works best. The central message to grasp is this: the clearer your mind is, the better your performance will be. Understanding this principle is central to gaining the competitive edge many elite athletes desire but lack.

Why is knowing how the mind works so vital to athletes, and how does such knowledge lead to improved performance? Since at a certain level of athletics, winning results from developing those six inches between your ears. Performance is improved by developing the mind.

Sports are simple. Here is what we do: we line up against the other team or opponent, and we compete. Competition lets everyone know who is in better shape. As two athletes compete, they begin to wear each other down physically. Once fatigue begins to set in, your mind begins to break down. First, your psychological defenses become compromised, and you begin to lose your ability to manage negative thoughts and feelings. You experience a mental mistake. This mistake can lead to conceding points to your opponent. As points are scored against you, you notice that your emotional energy begins to drop. Momentum is going against you. At this point, without a well-trained mind, your athletic performance begins to deteriorate quickly. Your mind begins to unravel. You feel frustrated, to the point of not wanting to care anymore about the competition. You still compete hard, but not so hard that you would experience a public "mental breakdown." This is challenging because many emotions are welling up within you at this moment. Your psychological defenses can't contain the many stressors you've been trying to block out. So you give up. You give in. You lose.

Athletes are dealing with emotional factors that, when acknowledged and addressed, can lead to better performance, in both athletics and in life. The problem is that many are likely missing this aspect of athletic training. Athletes are often so focused on the performance—on wins and losses and all the other physical aspects of the performance—that they miss a key element needed to reach peak performance and success: managing the emotional side of sports. If an athlete can learn how to keep psychological defenses strong and the mind clearer, he or she can perform better.

Below the Surface

Have you seen the movie *Titanic*? When the *Titanic* hit the iceberg, at first it did not seem that the iceberg did much damage. That is because most of the iceberg was below the water line. The damage was not visible; it was deep below the surface of the water. However, you probably know that the iceberg caused major damage, and the *Titanic* sank.

The concept of the iceberg is a great analogy for the mind. Everything above the water line is the *conscious* mind. It represents only about 10% of the iceberg. The other 90% of the iceberg is referred to as the *subconscious* mind. The water line represents *psychological defenses*, as shown in the diagram on the next page.

A *psychological defense* is your mind's ability to block content in the subconscious mind from reaching the conscious mind. This allows you to better concentrate on whatever requires your focus at the present moment. Psychological defenses can be things such as denial, compartmentalization, and repression. For example, *repression* is a reflexive psychological defense that our brains use to block unacceptable thoughts, feelings, and impulses out of the conscious mind. Psychological defenses function as protection in certain ways. Other psychological defenses include intellectualization, rationalization, or reaction formation. Knowledge and education can also offer strong psychological defenses. As you are learning about the way the mind works, you are building up your defenses. Knowledge is power.

The conscious mind includes those things you are consciously aware of—for example, the noises you hear, the words you are reading, and your current environment. You live in a culture that constantly tries to capture the attention of your conscious mind. Each day, you move quickly from one external stimulus to another—rushing to get ready for school, moving from class to class, going to practice, eating dinner, studying, and watching television. In the quieter moments between this rushing, you likely engage your conscious mind by looking at your smartphone. A recent study in the *Journal of Behavioral Addictions* stated that female college students spend up to ten hours a day on their phone and that males spend nearly eight hours.[6] Your conscious mind is likely bombarded with stimuli throughout your entire day.

Three Parts of the Subconscious Mind

The *subconscious* is a term used to describe everything below the "water line." The subconscious mind is composed of three parts that can be viewed as three levels: the *preconscious* mind, the *exconscious* mind, and the *unconscious* mind. Let's look at these three parts in detail, including life experiences represented as red dots. The diagram below shows all of the parts of the mind in the context of our iceberg example.

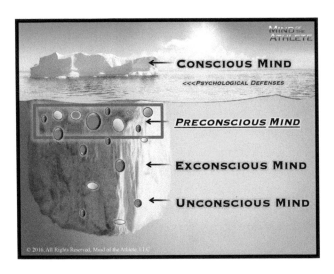

The Unconscious Mind

The *unconscious* mind is a term used by Sigmund Freud, an Austrian neurologist who became known as the father of psychoanalysis. He was a physiologist, medical doctor, psychologist, and influential thinker of the twentieth century. Much of this iceberg model of the mind, especially the unconscious mind, is a significant part of Freudian psychoanalysis. Essentially, the concept is this: your unconscious mind stores many past experiences that are either too threatening, too emotionally charged, or seemingly not needed for you to excel or thrive. Thus, these memories are stored deep within your unconscious mind.

You likely do not remember much before the age of five, but you have five years of memories from that time. Where are they? They are stored in your unconscious mind. Perhaps you have encountered certain traumatic events in your life, but those experiences are fuzzy, vague, and difficult to recall fully. Those memories and various aspects of the experiences are stored in your unconscious mind. Sometimes, they are deeply buried in the unconscious mind to protect us. Such memories can sometimes be brought up into the conscious mind. One way to do this is through the process of psychoanalysis. In a safe, confidential, trusted therapeutic relationship with a trained professional, a person may be able to bring to their conscious awareness a memory from their unconscious mind. Most of the time, though, these memories remain unconscious. Yet memories play a significant role in life because they are the building blocks for constructs such as trust, self-soothing, and attachment. Think about the house you live in. Although you can't see the concrete foundation of your home, it directly impacts everything that rests on it. This is also true with the unconscious mind.

The Exconscious Mind

The middle part of the subconscious mind is the *exconscious* mind. This is a term I coined to describe the place in your mind where outdated or less useful memories are stored. For example, think about a favorite birthday. This memory is stored somewhere in your mind. It may take some time for you to identify memories from the exconscious mind that are associated with that special occasion. But as your memory travels upward through your preconscious mind, through your psychological defenses, and into your conscious mind, recollection will become clear. You can access such memories in your exconscious mind, but it may take a little time to do so. Seeing a picture, hearing a song, or smelling a scent may help bring up a memory from your exconscious mind. Athletes store many memories of past athletic practices and competitions. When you are able to access this treasure trove of past experiences more easily, it can help your athletic performance tremendously.

The Preconscious Mind

Of the three parts of the subconscious mind, the *preconscious* mind is the most important in achieving high performance. This is the place in your mind where memories are stored that you can recall easily but are outside of your immediate awareness.

The preconscious mind is like a back burner on a stove. When

> The preconscious mind is the place in your mind where memories are stored that you can recall easily but are outside of your immediate awareness.

you cook you tend to place the pots and pans that you are working with on the front burners. It's easier to physically work with them there. But the other food that you are not directly handling at the moment can be placed on the back burner. While it's a bit more out of the way, you are aware of this food. You'll leave it there for a while until the time is right to re-engage it. Like rice simmering on the back burner of a stove, so too are things in your preconscious mind.

As you go through your day, you are continually processing new information through your conscious mind, and it ends up in your preconscious mind. Located in your preconscious mind are all the things that happen to you that you are not currently dealing with. What went on in practice today? How did you do in last week's game? Many of these thoughts are about events of the past. Some are events of the future. Do you need to study for a big test? Will your sore ankle or injured shoulder heal in time for the next game? Will you have another blissful moment of getting a kiss from that person you like? Your psychological defenses are trying to block out these thoughts so you can stay in your conscious mind and deal with whatever needs your immediate attention.

Often, the material in your preconscious mind is made up of unresolved, emotionally charged life experiences—both positive and negative. We tend to process the negative life events more frequently. But you may also notice that after a great performance, you find your mind continually drifting back to replaying those moments. In fact, sometimes a great performance can be as distracting as a bad performance because your mind replays it too much. The mind wants to resolve these emotionally charged and unresolved memories in your preconscious mind.

There is often more content in your preconscious mind than you realize. You become more aware of what is in your preconscious mind when the busyness of life slows down and your conscious mind takes a break. You become more aware of what is in your preconscious mind when you are putting your head on your pillow and trying to fall asleep. Can you recall a time when you tossed and turned while lying in your bed, thinking about random things you did not have time to concentrate on during the day? Where are those thoughts coming from? Have you ever driven in a car and simply drifted off into deep thinking, with unintentional thoughts slowly coming to your mind? These thoughts come up from your preconscious mind and enter your conscious mind. Many athletes say they do their best thinking when they are running; that's when they become more aware of what is in their preconscious minds. Daydreaming in class is yet another time when the content in the preconscious mind drifts up into the conscious mind.

One important characteristic of the preconscious mind is that time does not have any meaning there. You may have memories in your preconscious mind from several years ago. Such memories are often traumatic. The feelings from an event may be quite intense as soon as you think about it. It may have occurred years ago, but to you, it feels like yesterday. This is why many older athletes can vividly describe significant life experiences in sports from long ago.

The preconscious mind is very important in performance because the clearer it is, the better you will perform. When the preconscious mind is clearer, productivity increases, focus becomes sharper, and your energy level is heightened. Your mood tends to be more consistent and more positive. Time management improves, and your interpersonal skills are strengthened. Think of how you have felt after a relaxing vacation or after you have taken some time off and then returned to your regular school work or training. You probably had a little extra pep in your step, more energy, and an improved sense of humor. A clearer preconscious mind leads to all of these positive attributes. Unfortunately for many people, especially dedicated athletes, the preconscious mind is flooded.

The "Dots" That Cloud Your Preconscious Mind

In psychology, we often use the concept of "dots" to represent emotionally charged life experiences in a visual way. There are four main negative emotions that you likely struggle with:

1. Anger
2. Depression
3. Hate
4. Anxiety

The stronger these emotions are, the more time you are likely to spend thinking about the life experiences that led to your feeling of these emotions. These negative emotions also have a way of draining our energy quickly—you may be physically in great shape but emotionally drained. As you can see in the next diagram these "dots" flood your preconscious mind.

It is important to be able to understand these four emotions so that you can manage them effectively. I like short, concise, and simple definitions for complex things. Thus, I tend to avoid "psychobabble," which can be common in my field of psychology. One of my mentors, John Bisaha, taught me a lot about the psychology of these emotions. I am happy to share with you some of what he taught me. Here is an overview of these four emotions, in everyday language.

1. Anger

Anger is emotional hurt. When you are angry, you are really hurting emotionally. But it is likely that you do not have the vocabulary to describe your negative feelings of hurt accurately. Like many in the sports world, you probably were not taught many words to describe your feelings of hurt. Instead, you just suppress the hurt—stuff it down inside of you. What you do express are the symptoms of anger, which is the socially acceptable negative emotion to show in sports. Sometimes, anger is even encouraged or reinforced.

Imagine saying to your coach what you are really feeling and using proper vocabulary (words) like this: "Coach, I felt belittled in front of the team when you spoke to me with that condescending tone of voice and chastised my effort." What do you think your coach would say in response to such wording? If you want to resolve feelings of emotional hurt more effectively, it is helpful to begin to label your feelings better. For example, if you know that you feel hurt because you are feeling rejected, then you can work on figuring out a way to resolve the feelings of rejection.

Anger can be experienced in many ways and at many levels. How you experience anger may be different from your teammates. Some athletes need to yell while others may become withdrawn yet intense. Sometimes a small dose of anger may be a good thing. For example, it can be utilized to help you shift into a more competitive, aggressive mindset. One athlete I served would visualize her critics saying negative things about her just to get her fired up for the start of a game. This often works well for many athletes. Yet, while anger can be a good spark, it can also be a bad fuel. Because anger draws from a well spring of negative emotions, it is difficult to compete for a long time in this mindset. It can be too emotionally draining. It takes time to learn how to use anger to your advantage to help you compete better. Over time you will figure out what works best for you.

Many famous athletes have been required to undergo anger management as part of their rehabilitation process following an incident in which the law, league policy, and/or team rules have been violated. What they are really undergoing is emotional hurt management.

In a lighthearted yet meaningful way, the 2003 movie, *Anger Management* starring Adam Sandler and Jack Nicholson, revealed this problem. Sandler's character, Dave Buznik, receives anger-management training from Nicholson's character, Dr. Buddy Rydell. Dave learns to recite the word "goosfraba," a term used by Eskimos to calm their children, when he is getting angry. There is a scene at Yankee Stadium, when Derek Jeter turns to Roger Clemens and says, "Goosfraba," to which Clemens utters it back. While initially feeling alone in his journey undergoing anger management, Dave later learns that Dr. Buddy has actually helped many people, including famous athletes like Jeter and Clemens. While fictional, the movie did tear down some stereotypes about men and athletes developing skills to better manage their feelings. This movie reiterated the point that anger management really is about emotional hurt management. I suggest that you watch this movie, or watch it again, and note the psychology woven throughout the story.

2. Depression

Depression is hurt held inward. When we hold in our emotional hurt, we are going to either implode (collapse inward in a sudden or violent way) or explode (act out in a sudden or violent way). Neither of these options is optimal. While exploding may be an easier response to feelings of emotional hurt, it can lead to further problems.

> **Depression is hurt held inward.**

Imploding is more common. The problem is that the more we hold in our emotional hurt, the more depressed we feel. These symptoms include lethargy, decreased motivation, negative thinking, social withdrawal, diminished interest in things you used to like, agitation, irritability, insomnia (the inability to fall asleep and/or stay asleep), and changes in appetite. In advanced cases, you may begin to have thoughts about whether or not you even want to continue living. Such situations are to be taken seriously because, according to the Centers for Disease Control, suicide is the second leading cause of death for people who are ten to twenty-four years old.[7] If you or a teammate feels suicidal, the National Suicide Prevention hotline is 1-800-273-8255. Call it immediately, or ask someone else to. Please know that there is always hope and help available.

According to the American Psychiatric Association, women are "nearly twice as likely" as men to develop depression, anxiety, and eating disorders. In fact, anorexia and bulimia are twice as common among athletes as in the general population of women, according to the National Association of Anorexia Nervosa and Associated Disorders (ANAD). Women are expected to gain muscle in training but stay thin to uphold a standard of beauty outside of sports. That isn't possible! Anorexia and bulimia have the highest mortality rate of any mental illness, according to ANAD. More women have eating disorders than breast cancer, yet every major women's and men's sport has a pink-ribbon campaign, while mental health issues go less noticed.[8]

Eight-time Olympic medalist Allison Schmitt, a swimmer, struggled with post-Olympic depression after returning from the London 2012 Olympic Games with five medals. It took her two years to talk about it publicly. Then in May 2015, Schmitt's first cousin, a female Division I basketball recruit, committed suicide. That tragedy propelled Schmitt to speak out about depression among athletes and encourage them to seek help. She said, "I know it's not easy to ask for help, but it's OK to do so."[9] I applaud Allison for her decision to share her story because it helps destigmatize depression among athletes.

Dwayne 'The Rock' Johnson is one of the toughest people I've ever met. He, too, has struggled with depression. In an interview on Oprah's Master Class, Dwayne disclosed, "I found that with depression one of the most important things that you can realize is that you are not alone. You are not the first to go through it. You are not going to be the last to go through it. Often times it just happens. You feel like you are alone. You feel like it's only you. You are in your bubble. I wish I had someone at that time who could just pull me aside and say 'hey, it's going to be okay.' You just have to remember to hold on to the fundamental quality of faith. Have faith that on the other side of your pain is something good." No matter who you are or how tough you may think you are, depression can impact your life.

3. Hate

Hate is a strong feeling that many athletes often use in their everyday vocabulary: "I hate her" or "We hate that team." Whenever you want to use the word "hate," substitute the words "feeling threatened by." What you are really saying is, "I feel threatened by her" or "We feel threatened by that team." In the example of the girl, you might feel threatened because she has the potential to take your starting spot, knows a secret about you, or maybe even has expressed interest in the person you are dating. Ouch! Now it makes sense why you "hate" her.

Feeling threatened by another person can bring about a wellspring of negative emotions that are counterproductive to long-term, sustainable, high performance. Incidents such as bullying and hazing among athletes can warrant strong feelings. According to a 2014 study by researchers at Alfred University in New York, hazing is no longer a problem confined to colleges and universities. They found that hazing is becoming more frequent and more violent in high schools, with more than two million students experiencing hazing each year.[10]

Bullying is typically verbal and/or physical aggression that is meant to harm a person psychologically or physically. *Hazing*, on the other hand, involves behaviors that are more about maintaining traditions or hierarchy. It can be a group initiation rite that gets out of control and causes significant and lasting psychological and/or physical harm to the victim.[11]

According to a 2014 study, 71% of those who are hazed suffer from negative consequences, ranging from sleep problems and decreased self-esteem to depression and post-traumatic stress disorder.[12]

Do your best to eliminate the threats in your life in a constructive way, or at least try to manage them better. This is not a simple task. Rivalries in sports can teach you a lot about managing hate toward an opponent.

In the town of Phillipsburg, New Jersey, where I grew up, we have a longstanding rivalry with Easton, Pennsylvania. The annual Thanksgiving Day football game has been played for 109 years, typically in front of groups of more than 15,000 fans. An ESPN commentator said during the station's nationally televised broadcast of the 1988 game that the water in the Delaware River that separates the two communities is thicker than the families' blood. It is common to hear players, and fans, on both sides say, "I hate Easton" or "I hate Phillipsburg." That is because the threats are quite real when competing against each other, such as experiencing the deepest agony of defeat of one's season. Interestingly, through these great competitions and often after graduating from high school, many of the athletes from both communities become close. Former PHS quarterback John Troxell told a reporter, "Guys who play and have played in this game, both for P'burg and Easton, become like family." They actually understand the rivalry in a more transcendent way. The hate diminishes. The love begins to replace it. Sure, those feelings of hate can reemerge on game day, but mostly in a playful way for the fans. The life lessons learned from such a rivalry really do teach us how to better manage our feelings while keeping sports in their proper perspective.

4. Anxiety

Anxiety is fear of the unknown. When there are unknowns in your life, it is normal and natural to feel worried. In your world of constant pressure to perform as a student athlete, every day there are significant unknowns. How am I going to get time to study for that test? Is my ankle going to heal in time for this weekend's game? Will my mom stop complaining about my grandmother? Who will I hang out with at the party? Such unknowns can bring about symptoms of restlessness, insomnia, increased heart rate, fear, dry mouth, "butterflies" in your stomach, and sweating. In this fast-paced, overscheduled sports world we live in with emotionally enmeshed parents yelling from the sidelines, performance anxiety is visible everywhere.

Jayden (all names have been changed to protect confidentiality) was an outstanding college football player I treated for anxiety at my office. Although he felt symptoms of anxiety throughout high school, he successfully managed the anxiety without treatment. But when he arrived for preseason football his freshman year, the symptoms quickly became overwhelming. It was more than he could bear on his own. I shared with him that it is quite common for incoming freshmen to struggle with anxiety the first few months as they go through the process of making the many unknowns known. We worked on developing skills to manage the symptoms of anxiety when they arose. Like many freshmen, he continued to struggle through the first semester. But I am happy to say that after that his symptoms subsided, his confidence grew, and the rest of his college academic and athletic journey was outstanding!

"Dots" represent many other emotions, but anger, depression, hatred, and anxiety are the most common. These emotions almost always involve some type of complex interpersonal dynamic with another person such as a coach, teammate, or parent. Maybe there is a special someone you care for deeply, but you are unsure if that person feels the same way about you. The dynamics between athlete and parent can be complicated and stressful, too. Or a recent spat with a sibling or friend may be wearing on you. Could the relationship with a coach or teammate be of concern to you? Playing time, an injury, or the fear that you may be underperforming can all dwell in your preconscious mind. The reality is that you will always feel these emotions in life, but the goal is to manage them better so that you can decrease the frequency, duration, and intensity of their presence in your mind. The harsh truth is that you and your teammates likely feel stressed too often, for too long, and too intensely. Your preconscious mind is flooded.

A Flooded Preconscious Mind Creates Emotional Stress

A flooded preconscious mind is the root cause of your stress. As an athlete, you've been trained to evaluate yourself relentlessly and critically and to constantly strive for more. Nothing ever seems good enough. You may even have become harder on yourself than any coach or parent. As a result, you "do" more. But the more you do, the more you realize how much really can be done. But for what? This has been called "The Race to Nowhere." It's a mass paranoia in sports that drives everyone to the brink mentally. The flooded preconscious mind becomes chronic.

Picture a full soda can. At first, if you squeeze the can with your fingers, there is some wiggle room. But if you shake the can, it quickly becomes very hard. If you were to open the tab, the soda would explode from the can. The tension experienced from a flooded preconscious mind is similar to the tension that builds up in the shaken soda can.

Emotional pain often manifests, or shows up as physical symptoms. Think of a time you were emotionally stressed. It is likely that a part of your body also felt that stress. For many people, the place where emotional stress manifests itself is in the neck and shoulder area. If you were to squeeze those muscles, you would notice that tension has built up there, just like in the soda can. As an athlete, emotional stress often finds its way to your current or worst injury and amplifies those symptoms.

Under stress, you regress. You may be chronologically one age, but you act like a person who is a lot younger—whining, complaining, and acting selfish, irrational, or immature. Why? The flooded preconscious mind is eroding your psychological defenses. Your defenses are crumbling. The content in the preconscious mind is threatening to come into the conscious mind. To stay focused on the task at hand, your psychological defenses must work harder now to block out all that content. It is during these times that stress has a huge impact on you. For example, you may try to focus on an exam you are taking, what the teacher is saying, or a skill the coach is helping you refine; however, with a flooded preconscious mind, you can't concentrate well. It is almost as though the brain just stops working.

It doesn't matter how much money you have, how much fame you have experienced, or how great an athlete you are. None of these things seem to make a difference if the preconscious mind is flooded; the outcome is the same. When the preconscious mind is flooded, emotional regression occurs—for everybody. Even our best-trained soldiers can be in a stressful combat zone for only so long, and then we have to remove them from their tour of duty because their psychological defenses get eroded and their preconscious minds get too flooded. You don't need to look hard within the sports world to see a stressed-out grown man acting like a spoiled brat. He may be a twenty-eight-year-old professional athlete behaving like a fourteen-year-old again. The athlete loses sight of key lessons and maturity previously learned. It is unfortunate, but you can probably think of a person in your own circle of life who has fallen from grace. If the athlete's private life is revealed, it will likely be discovered that he or she was under incredible stress at the time.

The next diagram shows how stressful experiences result in many "dots" flooding the preconscious mind.

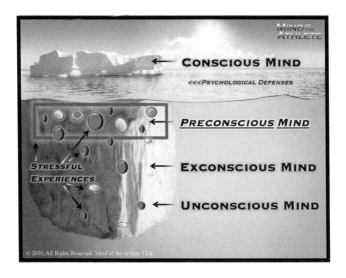

When your preconscious mind is flooded, you want to release the tension you are feeling in your mind and body. Although there are positive ways to do this such as talking, exercising, or sleeping, there is a counterproductive way that athletes often release tension: using drugs and alcohol.

Using drugs or alcohol is a way many athletes self-medicate their feelings. One athlete told me she smoked weed in the parking lot every morning before high school just to reduce the feelings of anxiety she felt about performance. Another athlete told me that nearly everyone on his team smoked weed during the season, even before games, to relax. I wish they would study sports psychology more so they would have a better repertoire of mental tools to use instead.

On Saturday nights after a game, athletes often gather together and party. When they drink alcohol, it begins to break down their psychological defenses. Initially, this may help them let their guard down, become more talkative, and feel less stressed. But with increased consumption, their psychological defenses can come crashing down quickly. You never know what is really in another person's preconscious mind, but you are likely to find out quickly when alcohol is involved.

Some of the scenarios are probably familiar to you. First, there is that person who, with his arms snugly wrapped around your neck, says something like, "I love you. Seriously, man. I really love you. We've got to hang out more." Someone else gets "beer muscles" and wants to fight somebody. Another person gets happy feet and starts dancing with everyone at the party. The music is on, and the feet just start moving. There is also that person who doesn't care who it is, but he or she is going to leave the party with somebody, and anybody will do. Finally, there is that friend or teammate who becomes emotional and sappy and starts crying. All his emotional baggage comes to the forefront, and the next thing we know, he is calling an ex, telling her how much he still loves her. These scenarios never end well.

These are just a few reasons why avoiding drugs and alcohol is a good idea. It can be too emotionally taxing to deal with the results of a night of partying, and no one wants any of what is in the preconscious mind coming out in an unfavorable way. It is always important to be very careful with drug and alcohol use, but it is especially vital during times when you are emotionally vulnerable.

A 2014 study found that within the month just before being asked about their alcohol use, almost four out of ten high school seniors reported drinking some alcohol, and more than one in five had engaged in "binge drinking" daily in the previous two weeks. Drinking endangers adolescents in multiple ways, including motor vehicle crashes, which is the leading cause of death for this age group.[13]

According to the Centers for Disease Control and Prevention, alcohol is responsible for more than 4,300 deaths each year among underage youth. Even though drinking is illegal for people under the age of twenty-one, people aged twelve to twenty years drink 11% of all alcohol consumed in the United States, and more than 90% of this alcohol is consumed in the form of binge drinks. On average, underage drinkers consume more drinks per drinking occasion than adult drinkers.

As for drugs, by the twelfth grade, about half of adolescents have abused an illicit drug at least once. The most commonly used drug is marijuana, but teens can find many often-abused substances, such as prescription medications, glues, and aerosols, in the home.[14]

In addition to pressure to perform and burnout, athletes are also vulnerable to becoming addicted to painkillers when they are treated for injuries. A June 2015 *Sports Illustrated* article highlighted a vicious pattern developing within sports. There is an increasing number of athletes playing sports year round who are experiencing intense emotional pressure combined with serious overuse injuries that require medical attention. The prescribed painkillers that doctors give to athletes following surgeries are leading more athletes to become addicted. To cope with the pain after the prescriptions have run out, many athletes are abusing painkillers and using them as recreational drugs. But because the drugs are expensive, they often turn to a cheaper drug: heroin. Heroin use is a devastating path that is destroying the lives of athletes at an alarming rate. According to the US Substance Abuse and Mental Health Services Administration, 80% of all users arrive at heroin after abusing opioid painkillers such as OxyContin, Percocet, and Vicodin. While opioid painkillers can cost up to $30 per pill on the black market, heroin, which is molecularly similar, can be purchased for $5 a bag and produces a more potent high.[15]

Loaded Issues

It is sad to hear about another athlete experiencing an emotional breakdown. Such breakdowns can occur at home as the athlete cries in their bedroom, throws a tantrum in the locker room after a game, or maybe even does something embarrassing in public, such as engage in a verbal or physical fight with another person. When the preconscious mind is flooded and the psychological defenses are weakened, the recipe for such an emotional breakdown can reach an even more intense level because of something called *loaded issues*.

All of us have loaded issues—a lot of them. These issues are the past emotional wounds you've experienced. These wounds can become clustered together around a similar topic. For example, a loaded issue for an athlete may be about losing. Due to the negative way his father responded to him whenever he lost in the past, an athlete likely will get even more emotional than normal whenever he loses today—especially when he loses a really big game. The current loss actually hooks into past, repressed experiences about loss, and together, all of these "dots" come raging up through the psychological defenses and into the conscious mind as one big mass of overwhelming negative emotion. The diagram below shows how loaded issues cluster in the preconscious mind, clouding it.

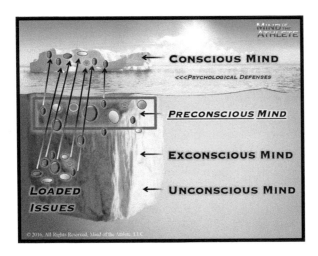

Often, it is not a pretty picture. An athlete might experience tears, swearing, violence, insecurities, fears, and more. For some, it can even be a fall from grace. There are many athletes who seemed to have it all together mentally, until one day it all came falling apart. Through the media, we eventually learn there was far more going on in his preconscious mind and that he struggled with some loaded issues. In the more redemptive stories, the athlete often then gets some professional help. Can you think of any professional athletes who have gone through this? Unfortunately, there are many.

> **There are many athletes who seemed to have it all together mentally, until one day it all came falling apart.**

Summary

The key to better performance is having a clearer preconscious mind. The problem is that most athletes have flooded preconscious minds. The preconscious mind is the top layer of the subconscious mind, followed by the exconscious mind and then the unconscious mind.

The preconscious mind is the place in the mind where memories are stored that you can recall easily but are outside of your immediate awareness. Unresolved emotionally charged life experiences, both positive and negative, occupy space in the preconscious mind. The four primary emotions you experience in the preconscious mind are anger, depression, hate, and anxiety. You become aware of what is in your preconscious mind when your conscious mind is less engaged and the content from the preconscious mind begins to bubble up through your psychological defenses. This often occurs when you are driving in a car, trying to fall asleep, or out for a long run.

Because time does not matter in the preconscious mind, it is important to deal with its content better so that you can have a clearer preconscious mind. As stress continues to build over time and fill up your preconscious mind, your psychological defenses become strained. Eventually, the tension in the preconscious mind, in conjunction with your loaded issues (past emotional experiences) from the exconscious mind, is more than the psychological defenses can manage. As a result, you experience an emotional breakdown.

PART 1:
KEY POINTS TO REMEMBER

1. You can improve your performance by developing your mind.

2. Athletes are often so focused on their performance—on wins and losses and all the other *physical* aspects of the performance—that they miss a key element needed to reach peak performance and success: managing the *emotional* side of sports.

3. The conscious mind, made up of everything you're aware of, represents only about 10% of your mind. The other 90% is the subconscious mind.

4. The subconscious mind contains three parts: the preconscious mind, which stores all the things that happen to you that you are not currently dealing with; the exconscious mind, which stores past experiences you can recall with some effort; and the unconscious mind, which stores many past experiences that are either too threatening, too emotionally charged, or seemingly not needed for you to excel or thrive.

5. The preconscious mind is the part that's most important to achieving high performance.

6. When your preconscious mind is flooded with either positive or negative thoughts that you don't deal with, your performance suffers because your mind isn't clearer.

7. A psychological defense is your mind's ability to block out certain thoughts so that you can concentrate on whatever requires your focus.

8. Stress breaks down psychological defenses, but drugs and alcohol break them down even faster.

PART 2:
CLEARING THE HURDLES

"The mind is absolutely instrumental in achieving results, even for athletes. Sports psychology is a very small part, but it's extremely important when you're winning and losing races by hundredths and even thousandths of a second."

—Michael Johnson, retired award-winning American sprinter

When an athlete's preconscious mind is flooded, five negative results tend to occur. Called the "five hurdles," they are the five mental obstacles that result from a flooded preconscious mind and block an athlete's ability to succeed fully, either on or off the field. These are the five most common psychological challenges I see athletes present with in my private practice. Recognizing these five hurdles and their causes is the first step toward experiencing a clearer mind and subsequently having better performance.

1. Insomnia

"Your life is a reflection of how you sleep, and how you sleep is a reflection of your life."

—Dr. Rafael Pelayo, MD, sleep specialist,
Stanford Center for Sleep Sciences and Medicine

The first hurdle is *insomnia*, which the National Library of Medicine defines as trouble falling asleep or staying asleep through the night. Episodes may come and go, last for short periods of time, or be long-lasting. Sleep-onset insomnia occurs when a person experiences difficulty falling asleep. Sleep-maintenance insomnia occurs when, after having been asleep, a person awakens and is unable to return to sound sleep. Insomnia is characterized by tossing and turning and thinking about things when you want to be sleeping. It has become a major concern for both high school and college athletes.

As a frequent speaker at high schools and colleges, I often give a workshop called "Sleep: The #1 Factor in Performance." I explain to the athletes that one of the first things I have to do as a psychologist when helping athletes is to make sure that their sleep is good. If it is not, then nothing else I teach them will be as effective. Sleep deprivation erodes even the most developed minds. I always ask groups of athletes how many of them have experienced insomnia in the past week. Usually, about 90% of athletes raise their hands, often with tired and frustrated expressions on their faces. They often lie down at night with the intent to sleep but find their heads filled with thoughts from their extremely busy day.

> **Many athletes' minds are overloaded at night because their days are often spent rushing from task to task, leaving no vital time to process their thoughts.**

Many athletes' minds are overloaded at night because their days are often spent rushing from task to task, leaving no vital time to process their thoughts. As a result, when the athlete finally slows down and puts his head on the pillow, he begins thinking about all the thoughts he didn't process during the day—the game, the test, the argument with dad, the text fight, etc. Has this ever happened to you?

This difficulty falling asleep and staying asleep that many athletes experience because of activity overload is the result of information continually piled into the preconscious mind. The preconscious mind simply cannot process thoughts as effectively in such an active environment, which is often from 6:00 a.m. until 11:00 p.m. This information builds up in the preconscious mind, causing it to become more and more flooded. When the athlete finally slows down at night and tries to fall sleep, he cannot because his conscious mind is bombarded by all the day's information from the preconscious mind. As he tries to fall asleep, stimuli from the external world around him halts, his psychological defenses relax, and the content in his preconscious mind begins to rise into his conscious mind.

Sleep is vital because it provides time for the conscious mind to shut down and allow the preconscious mind to go to work. Your preconscious mind uses sleep to clear out what is in it. Think of this as organizing your computer desktop. The preconscious mind reviews all the thoughts you had during the day and tries to examine your thoughts, file them away, and keep them properly organized in more specific "folders" deeper within your "filing system." When you wake up in the morning after a good night's sleep, it can be like seeing the desktop of your computer clear, organized, and with an inspiring image in the background once again.

According to the American Association of Sleep Technologists, athletes need even more sleep than the average person their age because their workouts require downtime to repair and rebuild their bodies after each intense practice session. In fact, the *British Journal of Sports Medicine* reported that 90% of overtraining injuries were caused by sleep deprivation. Good sleep can make a huge difference in performance, too. A 2015 study of the Stanford University women's tennis team found that ten hours of sleep per night over a period of five weeks resulted in improved sprint times and a 42% boost in hitting accuracy.[16]

Here are seven practical ways to combat insomnia:

1. **Keep a consistent sleep schedule.** Go to bed each night at the same time, and wake up at the same time. Ideally, these times should be in sync with your circadian rhythm—the natural time you fall sleep and wake up, feeling refreshed.

2. **Keep a one-hour presleep routine.** An hour before your ideal sleep time, begin to ramp down your brain. Turn off all electronics. Do not look at your phone. Do not play video games. Do not watch a movie or a game on TV. Stop studying. Take a bath or shower. Get into your pajamas. Have a light snack. Dim the lights. Read for pleasure. Talk about your day with a family member or roommate. Spend time in quiet prayer. As your brain activity slows down this way, you are more likely to drift off to sleep when you actually put your head on the pillow. This is what you did when you were a child, and you slept well then. Now you likely don't do any of these presleep preparations. Get back to this routine, and you can experience good sleep again.

3. **If you experience sleep-maintenance insomnia, do not get out of bed.** Although it may be annoying

to lie there thinking about your stressors, it is better to stay in bed. The reason is that once you get up and engage your brain in activity, it is less likely that you will be able to fall back asleep at all for the rest of the night. The next day, your performance will be significantly compromised. Instead, if you can stay in your bed, you are in a better position to catch another wave of sleepiness that will wash over you and help you go back to sleep. This wave may take one or two hours to come, but at least you will get back to sleep.

4. **Take out the mental trash.** Talk, write, and pray about the thoughts running through your preconscious mind. The more you can process them before lying down, the less likely you are to spend time thinking about them while your head is on the pillow.

5. **Do not sleep with your phone in your bedroom.** And don't look at it once you start your presleep routine. Like many of your friends, it is likely that you sleep with your phone in your room, maybe even in your bed. It is also likely that you are looking at it throughout the night. This is contributing to insomnia because the blue light that these electronics emit actually suppresses melatonin, the chemical in your brain that helps you fall asleep. Looking at your phone is like taking an anti-melatonin or an anti-sleeping pill.

6. **Keep a pen and notepad in your nightstand.** When you experience sleep-maintenance insomnia, write down the thoughts you are having. The next day, make it a priority to resolve those issues so that they don't rob you of your sleep again. If you don't

write them down, it may be possible that you will know you had insomnia but be unable to clearly recall what you spent so much time thinking about. These emotionally charged, unresolved conflicts in your preconscious mind need your conscious attention, preferably during your waking hours.

7. **Identify the most beautiful place in the world you can think of.** When insomnia occurs, imagine yourself in this place. Your thoughts may keep racing back to your stressors, but keep battling to shift your thoughts back to this place of relaxation, safety, and serenity. Focus your attention on the sights, sounds, smells, tastes, and feel of this place. The more you can engage yourself in this imagery exercise, the more it will help you stay relaxed. The more relaxed you are, the sooner you'll be more likely to fall back asleep.

John's Story

Like many coaches, John struggles with insomnia during the competition season. As a head coach for a top-ten NCAA Division 1 team, his mind is so brilliant and his heart is so caring that he can't help but think of the many past, present, and future scenarios that are happening to his athletes. This is especially true when his team is not performing well.

John told me that he would get up and "get work done" when he experienced sleep-maintenance insomnia. This would only leave him tired during the following afternoon, sluggish at practice, and then wanting to go to bed earlier. But going to bed earlier threw off his natural sleep cycle, and he would wake up in the middle of the next night feeling energized, but at the wrong time of day. Mixing in a hectic travel schedule, family responsibilities, and pressures to succeed, this cyclical pattern was literally burning him out.

The solution to the problem was to have him "stay down," meaning not getting up but rather lying in his bed during his bouts of insomnia. Once John began applying this technique, he reported a significant improvement in his overall mental health and performance. He still struggles with insomnia at times, but now he has the skills to manage it better. This has shifted the balance of power in his battles with insomnia.

2. Performance Anxiety

> "Every athlete acquires routines
> as a way to help control nerves."
>
> —Hope Solo, American soccer goalkeeper

The next hurdle resulting from a flooded preconscious mind is performance anxiety. According to *Medical News Today*, *anxiety* is a general term for several disorders that cause nervousness, fear, apprehension, and worry.[17] These disorders affect how we feel and behave and can manifest as real physical symptoms. Mild anxiety is vague and unsettling, while severe anxiety can be extremely debilitating and have a serious impact on daily life.

Before a big competition, it is normal and natural for an athlete to feel anxious. However, performance anxiety tends to reduce an athlete's ability to reach the optimal arousal level that is necessary for competition and essential for the athlete to thrive. Your hands become cold and clammy, your legs feel heavy, you have to urinate one more time right before competing, and the rest of your body may not feel quite right. Sometimes, when the competition begins, you are not nearly relaxed enough for your muscles to fire the way they should. So much blood has rushed into your internal organs for protection that the organs are under the "fight or flight" response to stress. The "fight or flight" response is your body's normal physiological reaction that quickly prepares your body to either fight (dealing with what's bothering you right then) or flight (getting away from the problem or enemy). As a result, there is not enough blood in your arms and legs to react quickly or perform at a high level. You know you have the physical skills to thrive, but somehow your body just isn't moving the way you trained it to.

The physiological impact of anxiety affects all athletes at some point in their journey. I had a conversation once with a Hall of Fame NFL player. He shared with me that he struggled with performance anxiety throughout his career. Before many games he would be in the bathroom vomiting just minutes before the game started. If performance anxiety can impact him, it can happen to anyone. No one is immune to the physiological symptoms of anxiety.

When the preconscious mind is flooded, it triggers your body's natural stress responses. It may not be one large stressor in your preconscious mind but rather the culmination of many smaller ones adding up enough to activate your fight or flight response. Because anxiety can be defined as fear of the unknown, it is understandable why you feel so stressed—there are so many unknowns in your life as a student athletc, especially during moments of high pressure. You may not realize just how much you've been keeping in your preconscious mind because as an athlete, you've been trained to suck it up, push through the pain, and ignore your body's warning symptoms. But there are limits to just how long a person can do this.

The mind–body connection doesn't distinguish well the difference between real physical threats to our existence and mental stressors that we magnify so they *feel* threatening. To you, the experience of getting a bad grade or striking out during the final inning of the championship game may seem quite threatening. When the preconscious mind reaches a level where it is so flooded that it cannot handle much more, the symptoms of anxiety you feel can reach a level of an anxiety attack. An *anxiety attack* or *panic attack* is defined as a sudden episode of intense fear that triggers severe physical reactions when there is no real danger or apparent cause, according to the Mayo Clinic.[18] An anxiety attack is scary. The experience can mimic that of a heart attack. Anxiety attacks will get your attention and let you know that you are in need of change, that you can no longer just proceed as you were. Your stress has reached a limit.

Anxiety attacks occur because of a flooded preconscious mind. Learning to recognize the signs and symptoms leading up to such an attack will help you avoid them. The ultimate solution is to keep your preconscious mind clearer. Along your journey in doing this, here are seven practical skills to apply when you are feeling anxious:

1. **Take slow, deep breaths**. Breathe in through your nose for four seconds, pause for one second, breathe out through your mouth for four seconds, and pause for one second. This inhalation/exhalation process will slow down your respiratory rate to about six breaths per minute, if done correctly. A person's respiration rate is the number of breaths taken in one minute. The normal respiration rate for an adult at rest is twelve to twenty breaths per minute. A respiration rate under twelve or over twenty-five breaths per minute while resting is considered abnormal.[19] Slowing down your breathing brings in more oxygen, which slows down your heart rate and, in turn, activates the parasympathetic nervous system. This system is responsible for physiological aspects of relaxation. Your heart rate slows, circulation improves to your toes and fingers, and ultimately you will perform better.

2. **Listen to the right kind of music.** To reduce feelings of anxiety before competing, you likely have a playlist of your favorite pump-up songs. The problem is that high-intensity music activates your sympathetic nervous system, which is responsible for go–go–go! Up until one hour before you compete, listen to some music that will stimulate your parasympathetic nervous system. This music tends to be much slower, with no lyrics. Think of instrumental music that is played at a spa or a nice restaurant. The artist I like most is pianist Danny Wright. I encourage every athlete I work with to have a playlist of his music on Pandora or iTunes. This music will help you relax.

3. **Avoid getting too amped too soon before competing.**
    Try to stay calm and relaxed until you are ready to get
    your heart rate up, break a sweat, and fully engage in the
    ramping-up process. It's about hitting the right intensity at
    the right time, as illustrated by the X (on the left side) on
    the performance-curve graph below. As stress increases,
    so too does your performance, to a certain degree. You
    want to compete within the optimal zone. However,
    many athletes lose too much energy being anxious before
    they even compete. As a result, they get fatigued toward
    the end of their competition. Instead, they should focus
    on staying calmer up until thirty to sixty minutes before
    competing. In addition to listening to relaxing music, try
    putting yourself in an environment that is not stimulating,
    negative, or intense. Move away from a parent who is a
    worrier, a teammate who mumbles negative words, or a
    coach who is angry. The more you make such adjustments
    to your precompetition routine, the more you'll conserve
    energy, maximize your output while competing, and
    avoid "tanking" in the end.

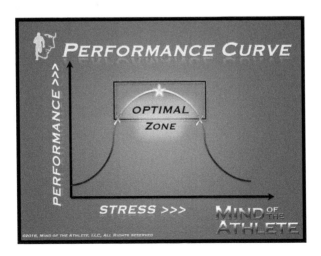

4. **Eat the right food.** According to a few nutritionists I know, an optimal food to eat is a peanut butter and jelly sandwich (with a glass of water) about one hour before competing. The reason is that this sandwich has the right amount of protein, sugar, and carbohydrates. But more importantly, it will dissolve in your stomach easily and quickly and thus require little blood to break it down further as it moves through your digestive system. Then you will have more blood in your muscles, where you need it more. Try this test to find out if the food you tend to eat before a competition can be digested easily. Place some of the food in a bottle of water, shake it up, and then see what it looks like in one hour. A PB&J sandwich will look like mush, which is what you want. But a Snickers bar or a piece of chicken (even though I enjoy them) would still look quite the same. Eating the right food may lessen digestive-tract symptoms of anxiety.

5. **Make the "unknowns" known.** Teams playing in the Super Bowl each year travel to the game location a week ahead of time. The reason is to lessen their anxiety by getting them acclimated to the environment. They need to find out what the locker room looks like, see the lighting in the stadium, locate the bathrooms, see how the mattress in the hotel room feels, etc. As you make more of the unknowns known, your anxiety will decrease.

6. **Focus on the optimal emotion for peak performance, which is excitement.** Although it is normal to be anxious before playing, you want to be more excited than anxious. The reason is that excitement is a positive

fuel source of emotions, while anxiety is a negative one. To raise your level of excitement, it is helpful to adopt an attitude of gratitude. The more you run through a mental checklist of the things you are grateful for (two legs that work, an opportunity to play, teammates who care about you), the more excited you'll become. It also helps to tell people, "I feel excited!" when they ask you how you feel about the upcoming game. This will become a self-fulfilling prophecy.

7. **Keep it in proper perspective.** You are playing a game. It's only sports. I know you think this moment means so much, and it does. But in the larger context of your life, it really doesn't. You are more than this moment. You are more than a student athlete. Later in your life, people won't really care about your athletic accomplishments, and they probably won't want to hear you brag about them. What people really care about is how you treat others, what kind of sportsmanship you display, and the effort you give. Plus, the unfortunate truth is that few young men and women will play college sports after high school, and even fewer will go pro. According to the National Collegiate Athletic Association (NCAA), of the nearly eight million students currently participating in high school athletics in the United States, only 460,000 of them will compete at NCAA schools. And of that group, only a fraction will realize their goal of becoming a professional athlete.[20] Keep the bigger picture in mind.

Claire's Story

I was serving an athlete who was competing at an Ivy League university. While the rest of her teammates were warming up and listening to the fast-paced, inspirational music from the overhead speakers, she was doing something different. She had her own headphones on. Claire motioned for me to come over to her. She placed those headphones over my ears. The music I heard was the soothing melody of a Danny Wright song. I smiled at her and applauded her for applying this skill. Claire was not going to actually compete for about another two hours. She was managing her anxiety through music. With such an openness to trying new techniques to improve her mind, it's not a surprise that she went on to become an NCAA All-American!

3. Low Emotional Energy

"Fatigue makes cowards of us all."

—Vince Lombardi, former head coach, Green Bay Packers

A third hurdle resulting from a flooded preconscious mind and likely to affect performance is a low energy level, specifically a low emotional energy level. Emotional energy is your psychological capacity to effectively deal with the immediate stressors in your life. Sports are more emotionally charged than ever before. This is one reason why you and your peers feel so tired. You may possess great physical ability, but you may not be as emotionally healthy. The relentless pressure to perform has you chronically seeking out time to rejuvenate yourself. In fact, 82.6% of college students reported feeling exhausted (not from physical activity) and 86% felt overwhelmed by what they had to do, in the last year.[21] Learning to recognize that your emotional energy is low will help you recharge and perform better.

> **Emotional energy is your psychological capacity to effectively deal with the immediate stressors in your life.**

Jaciel was an incredible athlete. He trained like a champion, putting in long hours of hard work, lifting and running. However, during a competition, in the moment of truth, he looked tired. He was in top physical condition, but he was running out of gas. What was going on with this athlete?

Emotionally, he was drained. In sports, the idea is to break your opponent. The goal is to break him or her physically, mentally, and emotionally. Do that, and you win. However, in this situation, Jaciel was unable to rely on his athletic preparedness for success. He was too anxious, too nervous, and outside distractions flooded his preconscious mind. These things were undermining his performance. For student athletes, it's not just about physical readiness, training, or nutrition. Emotional energy management is vital.

Your emotional energy level can be compared to the water inside a bottle. Every morning when you wake up, you have a certain amount of emotional energy that you can apply to all the activities filling that day. As you go through the day, you become drained. Little by little, you use up your emotional energy, and the bottle empties. On a day of competition, your performance suffers.

Often, athletes give the best of their emotional energy to school and sports. By the end of the day, when they get home, their emotional energy level is low or even depleted. The time they spend with family or roommates can often be difficult and strained. This is especially true following a competition. As an athlete, you put great amounts of energy into academics, workouts, and competitions. Many times, this leaves you drained. You may feel overextended, overwhelmed, and on edge.

As a tough competitor, you have given everything in your emotional water bottle to the competition, and now very little is left. You feel emotionally spent. This is to be expected. However, without awareness of a low emotional energy level, you can present yourself as less than you really are. Negative aspects of your character may surface, and you are more likely to exercise poor judgment in some situations. Relationships may fracture, and you may react in ways you normally would not. This is another reason it is important to recognize times of low emotional energy.

So how can you gain more emotional energy so that you can perform and interact at your full potential?

Regularly rate your emotional energy level on a scale of 0 to 100, with 100 being the highest. Consider a number in the 90s to be an A. Numbers in the 80s are a B, 70s indicate a C, 60s are a D, and anything below 60 leads to an emotional failure, placing you in deep trouble. The key number on this scale is 70. I call this the "tipping point number." Once you hit 70, your emotional energy begins to plummet. Your psychological defenses break down more quickly, you feel the emotions associated with the content in your preconscious mind, and you feel like you are quickly unraveling.

An athlete who is ready for performance should have an emotional energy level in the 80s or 90s. Her emotional energy level—the ability to deal with stressors, mental fatigue, and other obstacles—should be high enough to deal with all the things that may come her way that day, especially during the competition. If her preconscious mind is clearer, she'll use less emotional energy, attempting to block out thoughts and distractions so that she can focus on the task at hand. Competing with a higher emotional energy number than your opponents can give you a huge advantage.

Here are five ways you can manage your emotional energy better:

1. **Identify an unresolved, emotionally charged issue in your preconscious mind that is draining you of your emotional energy.** Acknowledge it. Talk about it, especially with another person who is involved. Get counseling if necessary. The sooner this issue gets resolved, the quicker you'll feel this drain on your energy subside.

2. **Identify ways you refill your emotional energy.** Who do you like to hang out with who actually makes you feel better? Where do you like to go that makes you feel relaxed and rejuvenated—your bedroom, a friend's house, a park? What do you like to do that raises your emotional energy—sleep, go for a walk with your mom, read the Bible? Go and refill your emotional energy with these people, places, and activities.

3. **When you are tired, get some parasympathetic nervous system activity.** You need to rest. Get some sleep. Watch a movie. Read a book. Take a walk. Say no to going out with friends.

4. **When your energy level is high, make the most of the opportunity.** You can expect better workouts, more positive thoughts, greater resiliency, improved ability to handle interpersonal tensions, and more physical energy. This is a time for you to improve and thrive. As you keep your energy higher, it can have an exponential effect on you. Better training contributes to greater confidence, deeper sleep, longer concentration while studying, better grades, and more wins.

5. **As iron sharpens iron, so one person sharpens another.** Hang out with positive people.

Alessandra's Story

Alessandra's injuries were depressing. After rehabbing back from one, she experienced another. This was taking a toll on her motivation to continue competing. She loved her sport, women's soccer, but was it worth it anymore? I encouraged her to take some time off to heal emotionally by stepping away from her training. She even followed through with my suggestion to take a vacation to the Caribbean. With time away, her preconscious mind gradually became clearer. Her body began to feel stronger because her emotional stress was no longer amplifying the physical symptoms of her injuries. When her emotional energy started to consistently be in the 80s and 90s for most of the day, she returned to training. Her mood was better, her mental resiliency was higher, and she was now playing at a high level. When she noticed that her emotional energy was dropping below 70, she would stop her training to avoid the negative psychological ramifications during her comeback. By regulating her emotional energy better, Alessandra's setback was truly just a setup for a great comeback!

4. Misguided Tensions

"People go down bad paths, and they make bad decisions, but it's always justified in their heads."

—Maisie Williams, actress, "Game of Thrones"

Hurdle number four is what I call *misguided tensions*. You don't have to look very far in the sports world to discover that athletes often release tension in unhealthy ways. Some of the most common misguided tensions include sex, alcohol abuse, drug abuse, gambling, fighting, and overeating. Can you think of somebody, perhaps even yourself, who has released tension in a misguided way? It probably caused regret, and maybe shame. It was likely out of character, and you or the other person never really understood why you acted that way. It is likely that the preconscious mind was flooded, and defenses became worn down. The emotional charge from inside had to come out in some way, and it was released in an unhealthy way. The tension that athletes experience from the sports they are playing, and life in general, must be released in some way.

While out for dinner at a restaurant, I once overheard a professional athlete say "I'm going to drink these feelings away" as he headed to the bar. Being a sports fan and knowing who he was, I knew that he had a disappointing performance that day. His statement is all too common for many athletes. The culture around you may even encourage you to party on Saturday night to let off some steam by drinking alcohol. This is always a risky decision. Tension may get released in a misguided way. Many athletes get tripped up over this hurdle.

Deion Sanders had it all, or so the world thought. He was one of the greatest athletes of all time. Not many people are able to excel in both professional football and professional baseball. That is, however, exactly what Deion Sanders did—he thrived in both sports. He had contracts worth huge amounts of money, incredible fame, and expansive notoriety. In his book *Power, Sex, and Money: How Success Almost Ruined My Life*, Sanders discusses how his contracts, money, and fame did not fill him up. One night, he experienced an evening of great despair and felt very empty inside. While out for a drive in one of his many sports cars, he thought about suicide. He considered driving his car off a cliff. He wanted out. What he wanted out of most of all was not his life, but feeling empty and lost. The world thought he had it all, but he felt empty inside. No amount of sex, drugs, food, violence, success, or money could fill him up. How could this be possible?

Blaise Pascal, a well-known French mathematician, physicist, inventor, writer, and Christian philosopher, called it "the God-shaped hole in your heart." This philosophy explains that there is a part of your heart that can be filled only by a relationship with God.

Deion Sanders said, "I had nowhere else to turn at that moment, but I reached out to God." This was the defining moment of his life. From there, God entered his life with one of His many promises, which declares, "If you draw near to me, I will draw near to you." In that moment, Sanders' life changed. He grew dramatically as a person, father, husband, and athlete.

Before that time, Sanders had been engaged in misguided tensions. He was trying to break his internal tension with the common behaviors that our culture often tells us will work. However, those ways do not often work. They alleviate tensions temporarily. Following the temporary relief, you wake up as empty as ever, or in some cases worse than ever.

Misguided tensions often result from a flooded preconscious mind. The preconscious mind is the back burner where those things you haven't addressed yet are stored. When the preconscious mind is flooded, it creates tension. Imagine the soda can again. When you shake it up, the pressure builds, and the can becomes agitated, similar to the human body. Emotional stress is manifested in physical symptoms. Necks get tight, stomachs ache, and back injuries flare up. Built-up internal tension must be released in some way.

You need a better outlet to "let out" the tension in a healthier way. One of the very best ways for you to let out the tension is by developing a hobby. A hobby is a leisure activity that you pursue for the enjoyment and pleasure of doing it. By regularly pursuing a hobby, you will positively and proactively alleviate tension in your preconscious mind.

Few athletes today have hobbies, mainly because they feel they do not have time to pursue a hobby. In addition, parents today often don't encourage athletes to invest in a hobby. I often ask athletes what their hobbies are during an intake evaluation at my office. I have to explain to them that a hobby cannot involve their primary sport. I typically receive blank stares indicating that they have no hobbies. I then ask both their mom and dad if they have any hobbies and if they enjoy doing a particular hobby with their son or daughter. As you might imagine, their responses are often pathetic. I encourage parents to find a hobby they enjoy doing with their kids because if all they ever do together is sports, then one day when it all ends, they will have little in common anymore. Parents need to model healthy outlets like having a hobby.

What is your hobby? If you don't have one, go to a hobby store this weekend and go shopping for a new one!

You may be surprised to know just how many athletes have a significant hobby. Here are a few:

Athlete's Name	His or Her Sport	His or Her Hobby
Alex Morgan	Soccer	Paddleboarding
Christiano Ronaldo	Soccer	Bingo
Lolo Jones	Track and field	Dance Dance Revolution
Mike Tyson	Boxing	Pigeon keeping
Ronda Rousey	Mixed martial arts	Pokemon
David Beckham	Soccer	Fencing
Larry Fitzgerald	Football	Photography
Bo Jackson	Football and baseball	Archery
Serena Williams	Tennis	Recording songs
Danica Patrick	NASCAR racing	Traveling

Greg Strobel, a former US Olympic Wrestling Coach, told me he required all of his wrestlers to have a significant hobby. He noticed that athletes training for the Olympics who did not have a hobby gradually became tenser, and their performance declined over time. If a wrestler could not identify a hobby, he'd teach them his hobbies of fly-fishing or carpentry. Strobel said, "The farther down the path of a sport a person goes, the narrower their life can tend to get. This can be unhealthy for various reasons. There is more to life than just your sport. Hobbies connect you with people from different walks of life, yet with a similar passion."

Here are four ways you can manage misguided tensions:

1. **Identify the most negative way you let out tension.** Acknowledge it. Own it. Take responsibility for it. Try to understand the origins for beginning this maladaptive pattern. Who modeled this to you?

2. **Identify the positive ways you release tension.** Ask yourself, "Why don't I tend to do this more often if I know it is good for me?" Think back to a moment when you did release tension in this manner. Why did it work?

3. **Grow your hobby.** Identify what your primary hobby is. Plan out some ways you are going to develop your hobby even more. Who are some people who share your same hobby? Contact these people and schedule some time to pursue your mutual hobby.

4. **Identify a person you'd like to emulate regarding managing tension.** Study this person. Find out how he manages negative emotions. Learn more about his coping techniques. What changes have made a difference in his life?

5. Loneliness

"It can be dark and lonely at the top."

—Victoria Pendleton, Olympic Gold Medalist, cycling

The fifth and final hurdle is loneliness. Athletes between the age of fifteen and twenty-five are more technologically connected than ever before. They have many friends on social media sites, but many of their actual friendships are shallow, and few other relationships are very deep. Your generation of athletes is more technologically connected, but more emotionally disconnected, than ever. When athletes are asked who they share their deepest thoughts, concerns, and desires with, most will admit that they feel very lonely. In fact, 60.6% of college students felt very lonely in the past year.[22] They are uncomfortable sharing information with many people because they do not trust that people will keep their personal information private. This is especially true for elite and professional athletes. As a result, many athletes end up feeling very isolated. They often feel as though nobody will understand what they are going through and that others will not understand or relate to the thoughts in their preconscious mind. Have you ever felt like you had no one to share your deepest thoughts and feelings with?

One indicator of this emotional disconnect is today's hookup culture. There once was a time when adolescents dated each other. Today, dating is much rarer. One definition of dating is getting to know another person, and then there is a sexual interaction. Hooking up is defined as having a sexual interaction, and then you may, or more likely may not, get to know the person emotionally. Research shows that students involved with this prevailing hookup culture have more depression. According to one multicampus study, college students who engaged in more hookups (casual sex with someone they had known for less than a week) had greater psychological distress. Those who had recently engaged in casual sex reported lower levels of self-esteem, life-satisfaction, and happiness compared to those who had not had casual sex in the previous month. And students who recently engaged in hookups had higher distress scores as indicated by levels of depression and anxiety.[23]

I read a quote from an anonymous person that said, "A relationship with no trust is like a cell phone with no service; all you can do is play games." It is likely that you, too, are tired of people playing games and instead want more meaningful relationships.

If you are struggling with symptoms of loneliness and/or depression, I want you to know that there is help and hope. There are people out there who have dedicated their lives to counseling. At the Mind of the Athlete company, we have a team of professionals who serve in this way. Across the country, there are thousands of counselors, therapists, psychologists, and coaches ready to talk with you. Break through the stereotype in sports that talking with a professional is a sign of weakness. Instead, ask your parents about the possibility of getting connected with a professional to begin this journey. It's amazing how talking about your feelings in a safe, supportive, and confidential environment with a person who "gets it" can make a significant difference in your life.

Here are four ways you can manage loneliness better:

1. **Know that you are not alone.** Feelings of loneliness and depression are far more common than you

realize. When you share how you are truly feeling, you will realize how many other people feel or have felt the same way.

2. **List some key people you can connect with.** Who do you feel comfortable with? Make a list of people that you'd like to spend time with and contact them. Identify the common interests you share, and find an event you can attend together.

3. **Learn the symptoms of depression.** Go online and read about depression. Educate yourself about depression. The more you understand how depression works, the more likely you'll be able to manage it better.

4. **Schedule an appointment with a counselor.** Go online to find a counselor in your area. Or call the Mind of the Athlete office at 610-867-7770. We will be happy to talk with you about how we can help.

My Story

I did not want to die. I just did not want to continue to live my life the way it was going. On the outside, everything looked great, and the world had no idea I was struggling so much emotionally. I was sixteen. I was an all-area football player, three-time class president, and captained my wrestling team to a state title. Yet throughout my junior year's football and wrestling seasons, I was experiencing extreme highs and extreme lows within my athletic journey. Emotionally, I was fatigued. But, I kept my true feelings hidden because I did not feel like anyone would understand.

My eighteen-match winning streak in wrestling had just ended in front of 3,500 fans during our rivalry match with the Easton, Pennsylvania, team. Despite leading by a score of 10–0, I tried a desperation move (rolling across my back while hitting a cradle) to pin my opponent in an effort to give my team a chance to win. Unfortunately for me, he caught me on my back and pinned me with three seconds to go. The fans went crazy! If I could have crawled under the wrestling mat, I would have. I was devastated.

As I was sitting on my bed crying that Sunday afternoon, my mother walked in and asked what was wrong. I revealed my true feelings to her. She was not aware just how badly I was hurting. How could she? I was an athlete and had been trained to hide my emotions well. Something desperately needed to change. And it did.

The first step was truly to admit that I was not superhuman. I was a person with feelings that mattered. I needed a break from sports, so I opted to not go out for the track team that spring. I became more active in my social life, and in doing so, cultivated relationships with some new friends who could relate to my struggles. Talking with them helped. They understood me. Eventually, much later down the road, I sought out counseling. I cannot express how beneficial this step was in my life. Loneliness ends when we receive the unconditional love, validation, and empathy that come from sharing our private emotional pains with another person. The power of talking about your feelings with another person is immeasurable!

Be careful about letting apathy set in—that feeling that you just don't care anymore. When you hold stress in your preconscious mind, it becomes overwhelming, and you develop apathy. That is when the emotional pain is so intense that you can't hurt or feel anymore. You say, "I don't care" and start to go numb. The terminology I use in counseling is that first we experience stress, then we begin to break down, and then we begin to break away. When we break away, we start shutting people out and going numb. That is a dangerous place to be.

Summary

The five hurdles are the five psychological concerns you experience most when your preconscious mind is flooded. It's important to understand that the underlying root cause of the five hurdles is emotionally unresolved, ongoing psychological stressors. A flooded preconscious mind may manifest symptoms differently for different people, but you'll likely experience at least one of these hurdles: insomnia, anxiety, low energy, misguided tensions, or loneliness. The more you understand the five hurdles, the better you will be at applying the suggested techniques for managing them.

PART 2:
KEY POINTS TO REMEMBER

1. When an athlete's preconscious mind is flooded, five results tend to occur. Called the "five hurdles," they are the five mental obstacles that result from a flooded preconscious mind and obstruct an athlete's ability to succeed fully, either on or off the field: insomnia, anxiety, low emotional energy, misguided tensions, and loneliness.

2. Recognizing these five hurdles and their causes is the first step toward experiencing a clearer mind and consequently having better performance.

3. Insomnia, which is the inability to fall asleep or stay asleep through the night, often occurs because athletes rush from one task to another without taking the time to process their most pressing thoughts during the daytime.

4. Sleep is vital because it provides time for the conscious mind to shut down and allow the preconscious mind to go to work. Your preconscious mind uses sleep to clear out all that is on your mind.

5. Anxiety is a general term for several disorders that cause nervousness, fear, apprehension, and worry, and it can range from mild to severe. Performance anxiety tends

to undermine an athlete's ability to reach the optimal arousal level that is necessary for competition and essential for the athlete to thrive.

6. Anxiety attacks can result from having a flooded preconscious mind.

7. Low emotional energy can affect an athlete's performance negatively. For student athletes, it's not just about physical readiness, training, or nutrition; emotional energy management is vital, too.

8. The tension that athletes experience from the sports they are playing, and life in general, must be released in some way. Sometimes they're released as "misguided tensions," such as sex, alcohol abuse, drug abuse, fighting, and overeating. Athletes often act out in these unhealthy ways because their preconscious mind is flooded with unprocessed thoughts, and their defenses become worn down.

PART 3:
RELIEF FROM THE FLOOD

"The moment I think about past letdowns or future hypotheticals, I mentally put myself on shaky ground. If I clear my mind of chatter, I can succeed, just like I did previously."

—Julia Mancuso, Olympic gold medalist, skiing

Clearer mind, better performance. This is the essential message. You must develop a pathway out of a flooded preconscious mind. You must be able to do it again and again and again so you can succeed and thrive without getting caught up by one or more of the five hurdles. Most athletes are so busy going through their days that they do not have time to take what is in the preconscious mind, bring it up to the conscious mind, and consider how it is affecting them. When asked how they are doing, most athletes will offer a cursory response—"Fine"— and move on with their hectic schedules, from class to practice to studying to hanging out with friends. They are not really dealing with anything in the preconscious and are unaware of its effect on their wellness or performance.

You work out your body in preparation for peak performance. Know and understand that you must also work out your mind. Follow these five steps, and you will be amazed at what you can do and how well you can do it.

Step 1: Be Aware

It's important to become aware of what is in your preconscious mind. Most individuals are not aware of what is in their preconscious mind because most do not even have time to think. Athletes, especially, do not have time to slow down or take a break. They are always off to the next thing on their list. Do you ever feel like you are too busy? Like most of your friends, you are probably overscheduled, overextended, and emotionally overwhelmed.

> **There is more going on in your preconscious mind than you realize.**

There is more going on in your preconscious mind than you realize. You can't just keep moving from one emotionally charged experience to another and think that those past experiences won't affect the present moment. You need to slow down and allow those preconscious mind experiences to arise into your conscious mind. When that happens, you will now be aware of what is really going on in your preconscious mind. Awareness occurs best when busyness stops.

Take some time to be alone—away from others and away from stimuli. There are many ways to do this, but an easy way is to go off alone for a walk. Take some alone time away from others and see what comes to your mind. Even if it simply involves lying in your bed for a predetermined amount of time without the lights or music on, take the time to be alone with your thoughts. See what emerges from your preconscious mind.

Another great way to raise your awareness about what is in your preconscious mind is to engage in a counseling session. In a safe, supportive, and private environment where your confidentiality is legally protected, you will have the opportunity to bring up those emotionally charged, unresolved experiences in your preconscious mind. As a psychologist, I often ask a person, "How are you *really* doing?" This is an invitation for the client to let down his defenses and allow the content from his preconscious mind to come up. It is a way of telling the client, "In here, it is OK to talk about how you are really feeling." It is amazing how quickly repressed content in the preconscious mind will surface. We always have a lot to talk about.

Awareness videos on YouTube are a great way for you to test yourself. One of my favorite videos is "The Selective Awareness Test" by Simons and Chabris (1999). In it, there are two teams of basketball players passing balls to each other: a team in white shirts and a team in black shirts. Those in the white shirts are passing the balls to each other, and those in the black shirts are passing balls to each other. These players move around and pass balls around in a confined area, making it confusing for twenty-six seconds. In a competitive tone of voice, I ask people to count the number of passes by the team in white shirts only. Afterward, I ask them how many passes they counted. The number they guess often ranges from ten to eighteen. The correct answer is fourteen. Then I ask the viewers if they saw a gorilla beating his chest in the video. "What?!" is the common response. I then show them the same video a second time. This time, they always see what they missed the first time: a person dressed in a gorilla costume walks among the players, stops, beats his chest, and then calmly walks to the left and out of view. Most people do not see the gorilla the first time. I didn't. And very few ever see the gorilla and count fourteen passes.

The point of the gorilla video is simple: there is far more going on in front of us than we realize. We need to be more aware. In the sports world, it is easy for people to miss things. All we have to do is sprinkle a little competition over people, and instantly they are focused on trying to get the correct number of passes, thus missing a gorilla. I often tell coaches and parents that the gorilla represents emotional health concerns of athletes. Athletes are crying out for help—right in front of the coaches and parents—and they are missing it. According to a 2013 study by the National Alliance of Mental Illness, only 7% of parents of college students reported their son or daughter as experiencing mental health issues.[24] Most parents are missing the gorilla—their child's mental-health issue—that is often right there in front of them.

The sports culture has long viewed mental-health issues as signs of weakness. Because of this cultural bias, athletes have quickly learned to hide any such feelings. So even if a person you know does not seem to show any signs of stress, don't be fooled. All of us, at some point, struggle with stress.

A powerful example of this is the tragic story of University of Pennsylvania's track star, Madison Holleran. As an ESPN online documentary, written by Kate Fagan, begins, "On Instagram, Madison Holleran's life looked ideal: star athlete, bright student, beloved friend. But the photos hid the reality of someone struggling to go on." Sadly, on January 17, 2014, Holleran committed suicide by leaping off a nine-story parking garage in Philadelphia. The people in her life were stunned, brokenhearted, and left to wonder how they missed it.

Become more aware of what is in your preconscious mind. I encourage you to ask someone you love, "How are you *really* doing?" I am hopeful that together we can raise awareness about the important issue of mental health among athletes.

Brandon Marshall's Story

When NFL wide-receiver and five-time Pro Bowler, Brandon Marshall, went public with his struggles of borderline personality disorder in 2011, many other players quickly came to him for guidance. "It started with someone telling their story, with someone breaking the taboo through daily conversation," said Marshall. The NFL player recognizes that being an advocate for mental illness is not easy, as it requires vulnerability. Marshall's troublesome past behaviors being publically disclosed have come with criticism. He has now become one of the most proactive mental health advocates in the United States, as he strives to be for mental health what Magic Johnson is for HIV. Marshall and his wife have created the Project 375 Foundation–Passionately dedicated to eradicating the stigma surrounding mental health by raising awareness and improving care for those in need. "Football is my platform, not my purpose ... I found there is more to life, more to me." Brandon Marshall is frequently sharing his story, raising awareness of mental illness, and empowering others towards getting professional help.[25]

Action Steps:

1. Take some time today to become aware of what is in your preconscious mind.

2. Ask a teammate how they are really doing. Be sure to let them know that you want to know and are genuinely there to support them.

3. Consider starting counseling.

4. Identify a person or people you believe will listen to you empathically.

5. Go for a walk in the woods. Get out for a long bike ride. Sit on a beach. Go for a long drive in the car by yourself. As you do so, you will become more aware of what is in your preconscious mind.

Negative emotions are often in the preconscious mind. It is important to be aware of some key emotions and what they may be linked to. Let's take a look at three of these negative emotions.

1. **Anger** is actually hurt, as mentioned in Part 1. If you are angry about something, you are emotionally hurting about that thing. In the sports world, there is often little support system or vocabulary that encourages or allows expression of negative emotions. It is awkward and uncomfortable to discuss with a coach or teammate a curt comment or action that caused hurt feelings. However, a hurt held inward for too long may become depression. As mentioned earlier, depression is hurt held inward. If you hold it in for too long, you

will implode, or turn your emotions inward, which is unhealthy. Holding it for too long may also cause you to explode, which is not healthy, either. If you are feeling some depression, it is likely that you have been hurting. Something is probably bothering you emotionally that you have been holding inside for too long.

2. **Anxiety** is another emotion we often hold in the preconscious mind. Again, anxiety is defined as fear of the unknown. When you are feeling anxious and filled with a tremendous amount of worry, it is likely due to too many unknowns in your life. As an athlete, you face many unknowns day after day, week after week. What is your next opponent going to be like? How will the next competition venue affect your performance? Will your injured ankle or shoulder hold up during the game? Situations that cause you to have anxiety are often unknowns that occupy space in your preconscious mind.

3. **Hatred** occurs when you feel threatened. When you feel hatred toward someone, it is likely because he or she has the ability to hurt you in some way. You may feel threatened by something that person might say to others that could impact your social status or playing time. Also, he or she may have the ability to hurt you by impacting your thought process and then clouding your judgment. Whatever it may be, you experience hate when you feel threatened by somebody.

Become aware of these strong emotions in your preconscious mind so that you can begin to recognize and minimize them.

Step 2: Process

Once you are aware of the material in your preconscious mind, you must process it. What does it mean to process? Essentially, you have to talk about it. It is not enough to just think about it again and again on your own, believing you can somehow resolve all of your conflicts by yourself. You may be able to resolve some of them, but most often, there is too much going on to clear your preconscious mind simply by thinking. Because the preconscious mind is flooded, you may not have the emotional and psychological skills to process all the material. Talking to somebody else can alleviate a lot of tension.

Do you have someone you can process the material in your preconscious mind with? Who do you talk to, confide in? To whom do you bear your heart and soul? Whose wisdom do you internalize? If the answer is that you do not have anyone, it is important for you to find someone. Try talking to a trusted friend, teammate, or parent. You may even want to contact a counselor, a therapist, or a sports psychologist. There is something mystical that occurs when you talk about your thoughts. Getting them out of your head and talking about them leads to a clearer mind and better performance.

Can you recall a time when you had a heart-to-heart conversation with someone? Have you ever shared something that was bothering you to the point that the conversation brought you to tears? It is likely that you felt much better after sharing. Sometimes conflicts cannot be resolved in the short term, but still, talking about them makes a huge difference. In fact, there may have been a time when you were discussing something and reached a point when you no longer felt the need to continue discussing it. It stopped bothering you. Talking about an issue disarms it. It takes the emotional charge off the experience.

Catharsis means a freeing of emotions. Talking about stressors is a powerful cathartic experience. One benefit of talking is that it alleviates the tension from those emotions in a positive, healthy manner. Repressed emotional stress can

> **Catharsis means a freeing of emotions.**

often manifest itself in a physical symptom, such as the pain sensations of a back injury.

You may have to fight against some untrue messages you've internalized about expressing your feelings. Talking about your feelings is not considered complaining, whining, or being a baby. It is merely expressing how you feel. New York Yankees star Alex Rodriguez professed, "Therapy should not be synonymous with a real bad thing. Kids need to know it is a good thing, that it is OK for them to seek help."[26]

Talking is most powerful when done in the presence of another person. Face-to-face conversations in which you can look another person in the eye have the greatest impact. Your generation often struggles with this skill. It can be hard for you to talk to a person directly about a concern, especially if that concern has significant interpersonal tension associated with it. In fact, most coaches tell me that the most significant leadership skill they need from leaders today is verbal conflict resolution. They need a person who can effectively resolve a problem with a teammate by talking to him or her in a manner that is productive, not destructive. Most athletes would prefer to text a person to resolve a conflict. But this mode of communication does not give you the ability to read the other person's visceral (gut) reactions or tone, and the conversation takes too long to unfold.

Military fighter pilots are masters at high-level communication, and we can learn a lot from them. After a mission or important meeting, they all remove their rank insignia from their military uniforms so they can speak more freely to resolve conflicts and clear out their preconscious minds. This exercise demonstrates the power of processing.

An article on the *Successful Meetings* website describes the fighter-pilot debrief as follows:

> The debrief must be a safe place where all team members—regardless of rank or seniority—are free to share their open and honest observations on how they and their teammates performed during the mission.
>
> In the military, we create that safe practice by stripping off our nametags and rank insignia at the beginning of the debrief (they attach to our flight suits with Velcro). With the nametags off, we create a learning environment where the sole purpose is to improve performance, both as individuals and as a team. Our goal for the debrief is to capture generic lessons and roll them into tomorrow's plan. Where appropriate, we will also disseminate those generic lessons to the rest of our squadron so that we can all benefit.[27]

The more you learn to talk about the material in your preconscious mind with another person, the better you will get at doing this. I often hear from parents of athletes I meet with for one-on-one counseling that a son or daughter is more talkative at home about her feelings than she is at school or with her team. Parents are often pleasantly surprised by their adolescent's comfort level in talking through tensions they have with him or her. Like an athlete lifting weights, you will get better at this skill the more you do it.

If you are not able or willing to talk about a conflict or concern, write about it. The more you write down, the better. *Journaling*—writing your thoughts and feelings down in a journal or typing them on your computer or tablet—has a profound effect on a flooded preconscious mind.

Every athlete I work with in my private practice or consulting gets a Mind of the Athlete journal. I encourage them to write down their thoughts and feelings in it. Sometimes we call this "brain dumping." The written content can be anything—it is just important that they "get it out" and can then have it in one place. One athlete I serve keeps his notes from each lift in this notebook. Another athlete makes lists after each game on the pros and cons of his performance. Yet another keeps detailed notes of his emotional energy throughout each day. Do you have a journal? If not, I encourage you to get one. Keep it in your book bag. I've been doing this for years, and it is a habit I find quite beneficial.

Your smartphone can also be a great resource for writing things down that otherwise would take up space in your preconscious mind. You likely have a notes section on your phone. Do you use it? I have pages for "blog ideas," a "to-do list," and "movies I want to watch." Create personalized pages like this for yourself, too. Also, your phone probably has a calendar. I encourage every athlete to get better organized by using this calendar. Put your entire athletic schedule and school syllabi into it. The more you write this material down, the less time you will spend thinking about it and hoping you remember it later. You can relax knowing that it is out of your head and written down.

A technique that is helpful to many sports teams is called "taking out the trash" before a competition. Players write down on a piece of paper all the concerns in their preconscious minds that they are unable to deal with at the time because they are about to go out onto the field. The act of writing allows them to acknowledge their thoughts. A trash can is placed in the center of the locker room. As the athletes leave the locker room, they tear the papers into little pieces and throw them in the trash to symbolically demonstrate ridding themselves of the trash in their minds. The athletes acknowledge that the trash is not going to help them excel in the competition, so they get rid of it. This allows the players to focus on the game, have clearer preconscious minds, and relax their psychological defenses.

Either talking about the content of your preconscious mind or writing about it will help you process and eliminate obstacles to your success.

Talking to a counselor can be extremely beneficial because that person is trained to know how to help you. As I mentioned earlier, counseling made a big difference for me. The athletic community is starting to make progress in removing the negative stigma associated with athletes who seek counseling. New guidelines released in February 2015 provide recommendations for high schools' health-care teams to recognize when high school athletes are experiencing mental health issues such as anxiety, depression, eating disorders, drug and alcohol abuse, and more. The ten recommendations encourage schools to have a plan that focuses on education, early recognition of potential problems, and effective referral to the mental-health system to help student-athletes, along with a plan to recognize and address potential crisis situations.[28]

Landon Donovan's Story

Landon Donovan, Major League Soccer's all-time top scorer (144 goals) and all-time assists leader (136), retired from professional soccer in December 2014 at the age of thirty-two. He has been outspoken about the lack of mental-health support for athletes. He said mental exhaustion forced him out of soccer for roughly four months, and he "questioned the overly macho aura that permeates professional sports." After battling depression during his career, he found respite in meditation and sought help from a therapist.

"We have a sort of stigma that being in a difficult mental place is not acceptable," Donovan said. "It's a little peculiar to me, that whole idea that if someone's physically hurt, we're OK with letting them take the time they need to come back, but if someone's having a difficult time mentally, we're not OK with letting them take the time they need to come back."[29]

Action Steps:

1. Start talking more about the content in your preconscious mind.

2. Experience the benefits of catharsis.

3. Fight back against negative internalized messages about expressing your feelings.

4. Develop the skill of talking, especially face to face with another person.

5. Be a better leader by developing verbal conflict-resolution skills.

6. Get a journal and keep it in your book bag. Practice the art of "brain dumping" by writing in your journal.

7. Use your smartphone's notes and calendar apps.

Step 3: Commune

Communing is connecting with something larger than yourself: a higher power, a greater authority. It is an important step that can be profoundly helpful to some people, while others may feel this step is not for them. Communing is accomplished by linking something in your mind that seems like a big deal to you with the bigger picture, therefore putting it in its proper perspective. Have you experienced concerns that seemed to overwhelm you, but when you compared them to the broader world, you realized they were not that significant after all? Some call communing self-reflection; others call it meditation. You can also call it prayer. Whatever you call it, that act of linking your concerns with something bigger than yourself is profound.

My former teammate and friend, Tim Longacre, once explained a great example of communing to me. He said, "Imagine you are out in the woods, all by yourself, sitting in a tree stand between four and seven o'clock in the morning as the sun is coming up in a perfectly still forest. That is when and where I do some of my best thinking. I am really able to clear out my mind. I can think more clearly. And as I do so, I am able to connect with Mother Nature, the universe, the Bigger Picture. The stressors in my mind seem to be placed in their proper perspective. As I leave the woods each time, I always feel better. My mind is clearer, and I feel more in sync with the world."

Meditation is an effective form of communing. A wise man once said, "Everyone should meditate one hour a day, unless he is stressed. Then he should meditate two hours." Do you meditate? Have you ever tried it? It is a great skill to develop. During my doctoral program in clinical health psychology, it was a requirement for us students to meditate as part of a class. We were studying the mindfulness meditation principles of Dr. Jon Kabat Zinn, professor emeritus at the University of Massachusetts Medical School. In the beginning, I struggled to sit comfortably for five minutes and allow my mind to be still. By the end of the semester, it was amazing how quickly twenty minutes passed, how much clearer my mind became, and how much better I felt.

Studies have shown that meditation reduces depression. Researchers at Columbia University found that regular meditation or other spiritual or religious practices guard against depression. The people who highly valued spirituality showed thicker portions of the brain cortex that may protect against depression, especially in those who are at high risk for the disease.[30]

Prayer is another powerful method of communing. *Prayer* is connecting with a power greater than yourself—most often considered to be God, however you may define God.

When you take the thoughts, concerns, and ideas in your preconscious mind and talk with God about them, everything is put into a bigger context. This helps you make better sense of the things that concern you. You can better understand them in the context of the long-run, the big picture. A 2013 Barna Research study revealed that 84% of Americans prayed in the previous week. According to another study in *The Washington Post*, 90 percent of Americans believe in God.[31] Consider where you are in that continuum. Are you praying at least once a day, bringing your cares to God and giving them to Him?

Research shows that praying can make a huge difference in a person's well-being. Stanford University Medical Center, *USA Today*, and ABC News conducted a study that discovered that prayer is tied with prescription drugs as being the most effective pain reliever.[32] Imagine that—prayer can be as effective as medication to relieve pain!

In a study of patients suffering from chronic pain, those who prayed daily reported a higher pain tolerance than those who did not. Although researchers don't yet understand how prayer can change perceptions of pain, they think its ability to foster a sense of spiritual support and therefore improve a person's mood may have something to do with how much pain the brain senses. Prayer also offers a distraction from pain, which is likely a component of how it provides relief, because it requires a person to shift focus away from what is hurting and toward something that is comforting.[33]

Identify a place where you can go to be alone with God to pray or meditate. Notice that as you begin to become silent, random thoughts begin to flood your mind. These thoughts are the material in your preconscious mind. You lose focus because those thoughts require attention you have not given them. You are too busy just trying to ignore the concerns, so they flood your preconscious mind.

Rabbi Alan Lew, author of *This Is Real and You Are Completely Unprepared*, explains prayer in his book in a way that I believe epitomizes why prayer is important in clearing your mind. He writes:

> "The thoughts that carry our attention away are never insignificant thoughts, and they never arise at random. We lose our focus precisely because these thoughts need our attention, and we refuse to give it to them. This is why they keep sneaking up on our attention and stealing it away. This is how it is that we come to know ourselves as we settle deeply into the act of prayer."[34]

It is so true! The thoughts that carry your attention away are those emotionally charged, unresolved experiences in your preconscious mind. They are not insignificant; they are deeply meaningful to you. Because of your busyness, you aren't able to process these experiences well. Whenever your mind is idle, you can't help but notice that you're thinking about these experiences again. Rabbi Lew was correct—when you pray, you find out quickly what is really in your preconscious mind and what is most concerning to you. You really come to know yourself better as you settle into the act of prayer.

Every morning before I leave our bedroom to start the day, I take some time for quiet prayer. I have a special prayer spot where I get down on my knees in reverence to God. It's in front of a window with a cross (I'm a Christian) sitting on the window sill. This time is important to me. It helps me slow down, express my gratitude for the many blessings in my life, pray for the people I will be serving that day, ask for protection for my family, and listen to the quiet whisper of God speaking to me. There are often things in my preconscious mind that only God knows about fully and can help me with; I surrender them to Him and take comfort knowing that He is in control. I typically conclude my prayer time reciting the words Jesus spoke in the garden Gethsemane: "Not my will, but Your will be done." Each time I get up off of my knees, I feel centered, relaxed, and ready to engage the world.

One of my favorite verses from the best-selling book in the history of the world, the Bible, says in Philippians 4:6–7, "Be anxious for nothing. But, in everything, through prayer and petition, with thanksgiving, make your requests known to God. And the peace of God, which surpasses all understanding, will guard your hearts and minds." This verse summarizes well what I experience through prayer.

You will find yourself, when at practice or trying to focus on something important, making mental mistakes because a flooded preconscious mind makes you unable to be fully present. This is how you come to fully know yourself as you commune. As you attempt to quiet your mind and commune, you will notice that many thoughts come racing into your mind. These thoughts seem like distractions. However, if you link those concerns to something bigger and commune about them, it will have a profound effect in clearing out your mind and ultimately will help you achieve better focus.

Stephen Curry's Story

As Golden State Warriors guard Stephen Curry led his team during the NBA Western Conference finals in the spring of 2015, the mainstream media reported his record accomplishments on the court. But Curry, the league MVP, said all the praise and accolades he received about his skills could never compare to his heavenly treasures.

The first time the twenty-seven-year-old player won the Most Valuable Player award, he publicly professed his faith. At the MVP ceremony, he said, "First and foremost, I have to thank my Lord and Savior Jesus Christ for blessing me with the talents to play this game, with the family to support me, day in, day out. I'm His humble servant right now, and I can't say enough how important my faith is to who I am and how I play the game."

Curry has also noted that about ten other players on his team attend pregame chapel services and pray together before games.[35]

Action Steps:

1. Identify a method of communing that works for you.

2. Decide on a time and place to practice communing.

3. Try to practice communing every day, consistently, for at least one week.

4. Try to build up the length of time you are able to spend each time in quiet communing.

5. Read some books, including ones by Dr. Jon Kabat Zinn, Rabbi Alan Lew, or the Bible, that will help you develop your ability to commune.

Step 4: Integrate

Once you have become aware of the thoughts that are flooding your preconscious mind, talked or written about them, prayed about them, or in some way communed about them, you must integrate them. Integrating is emotionally resolving the "dots" that were described in Part 1. When you've worked the material through enough that you no longer feel like giving it more attention, you've emotionally resolved it. The material sinks from the conscious mind, through the preconscious mind, and ultimately now resides in the exconscious mind, as depicted in the next diagram.

Integrating is an important step in clearing your mind. The material will sink down to the exconscious mind once it is resolved in a positive way. Integrating your "dots" well often requires another person's help. Integrating well is the art and science of good coaching, parenting, and/or counseling.

Have you ever been lying in your bed, crying because someone you loved broke up with you? Your mom may have been sitting on the end of your bed comforting you. As you vented to your mom, she likely offered you reassurance, warmth, and tenderness. Your mom may have even uttered such phrases as, "He is going to regret this one day," "You are too good for him," "There are other fish in the sea," and "He doesn't deserve you." Through her careful parenting of you in this situation, the emotionally charged experience was resolved enough that night to sink it to your exconscious mind. The next morning, you probably woke up feeling reinvigorated and ready to move on from him. You unfollowed him on social media, and deleted the pics of the two of you from your phone. This is a great example of parenting that helps you efficiently and effectively integrate a negative experience into your exconscious mind.

My high school wrestling coach, Bob Jiorle, once helped me integrate a traumatic moment well. When I was an untested sophomore in our first wrestling match of the season, I had to wrestle a returning state champion in a hostile away gym filled with 1,500 fans. Early in the first period, I shot in deep on the state champion, drove him out of bounds, and nearly took him down. The crowd went wild, thinking that I was going to give the champion a run for his money. Unfortunately, I think I just made him mad. Within a minute, he pinned me! I was crushed by my "failed" performance and by a missed opportunity to score big for my team. After the match, while I was gathered with the whole team, my coach transformed that negative experience into a positive one. He said, "Jarrod, if you can get in that deep on a state champion's leg, you will be able to get in that deep on anybody else you face this season." The coach reframed the situation in a positive way. After that, I really thought about it from his perspective. He was right. I began rethinking the match and quickly felt the emotional tension from this loss begin to subside. Coach Jiorle's comment also became a springboard for me to wrestle better every match going forward because I knew I could get in on anybody's legs.

Has your coach ever said something to you while on the sidelines of a game? What did she say to you? Great coaches are able to tell when you are struggling with negative emotions such as frustration, fear, or anxiety. They also have a unique way of alleviating those emotions on the spot by just offering a few well-chosen words. You may have then gotten a drink of water, collected your thoughts, and returned to the game with a better mind-set. One of the best coaches at doing this is Lafayette College field hockey coach Jennifer Stone. I've witnessed her do this again and again while I was serving as the team's sports psychologist.

Growing up, you may have been on the receiving end of some bad coaching. Too often I cringe while watching Little League sporting events when a coach escalates a player's negative emotional experience by shouting, "What were you thinking?!" or throwing his hat on the ground or walking away from a player who needs encouragement. When this happens, the player is left to deal with the negative experience that is now even more emotionally charged. I believe that this may be one reason why so many kids experience emotional burnout. John O'Sullivan, founder of the Changing the Game Project, stated in a recent TEDx talk about youth sports that 70% of all kids will stop playing sports by age thirteen.[36] A lot of coaches out there are doing more emotional damage than they realize. Have you ever had an experience with bad coaching? If so, talking this over with a sports psychologist can really help reframe the experience.

Unfortunately, some parents make sports a negative experience for their children, too. They want their children to win so badly—maybe because it's something they didn't get to do when they were children, or maybe because they are just extremely competitive—that they get angry with their kids—often in public—when they don't perform well. O'Sullivan, mentioned earlier, remembers when youth sports were about children competing with other children instead of adults competing with each other through their kids. After nearly three decades as a soccer player and coach, he began working to reshape youth sports and inspire a major shift in culture. That's why he founded the Changing the Game Project.

When I work with athletes in my private practice, integrating is what I help them do best. The art and science of good counseling is to help a person clear out those "dots" in his preconscious mind and have him now exist in his exconscious mind. Each time an athlete leaves my office, I want him to feel better because his mind is clearer. By offering solid science, knowledge, insights, and skill development, I also help athletes build up their psychological defenses. Ultimately, I am hopeful that they feel more confident so they can manage future stressors on their own. The following diagram depicts how a clearer preconscious mind provides room for your mind to concentrate on performance instead of "dots."

Another strategy that can help you integrate, or stay positive, is to consider carefully the people you surround yourself with and the influence they have on your life. Be careful whose counsel you accept. When you integrate negative thoughts and experiences back into your mind in a healthy, positive, and productive way, they occupy less space in your preconscious mind. This provides a great opportunity to thrive later because your mind will be clearer. That is the power of having good people around you. They can help you process negative thoughts and experiences in a positive way.

Tiger Woods' Story

At one point in time, Tiger Woods seemed invincible on the golf course. Many people said he was the most mentally tough athlete in sports. All of this came crashing down on November 29, 2009. Tiger's fall from grace has been well documented.

In the days and months that followed, Tiger immersed himself in inpatient and outpatient counseling. In his first interview after his extramarital affairs, Tiger explained to ESPN's Tom Rinaldi just how counseling helped him. Tom asked Tiger, "How well does the world know you?"

Tiger responded, "A lot better now. I was living a life of a lie. I really was. I was doing a lot of things, as I've said, that were hurting a lot of people. And stripping away denial and rationalization, you start coming to the truth of who you really are. And that can be very ugly. But then again, when you face it and you start conquering it and you start living up to it, the strength that I feel now, I've never felt that type of strength."[37] While there are ongoing struggles in his life, Tiger continues to be an advocate for counseling.

Action Steps:

1. Identify the people in your life who help you integrate material in a positive manner.

2. Schedule time this week to meet with one of these

people to work on clearing your mind.

3. Identify a person whom you can help clear his or her mind. Offer to help that person.

4. Think back to a stressful situation in your life. Identify the variables that led you to integrate this experience in a positive way into your exconscious mind.

5. Make a list of the positive people in your life you want to hang out with more. Make a list of the negative people in your life you should try to spend less time with.

Step 5: Perform at Your Optimum Level

The ultimate goal for every athlete is to perform well in competition. You can expect a better performance when you have a clearer mind. If you work hard at clearing out your preconscious mind and engage in this process again and again and again, you will successfully go out there and show the world all you have to offer. Inside of you is all the intelligence, creativity, passion, and energy you need to excel and thrive. You have the ability to focus and achieve your goals. All of this is already inside you. The question to consider is this: Is your mind clearer than it has been in the past?

When it is clearer, you can expect all of these positive attributes to flow through you. Your psychological defenses will last longer, and you will experience greater success. Realize now that your psychological defenses function like a permeable membrane. With a clearer preconscious mind, your defenses allow more of the positive qualities within you to pass freely into your conscious mind. You can use all you have inside you to succeed. You will feel more alive and more excited. When competing, you will be more in the moment.

Think of a time from your own experiences when your mind was clearer and you had a great performance. Think of those professional athletes who did all the right things, had a clearer mind, and thrived. Perhaps you, too, have performed at that level and won the championship. You possess all the skills. The question is this: Can you create the right conditions to do it again and again and again? Will you move through these five steps and achieve a clearer preconscious mind?

Consider the acorn. It is small, but everything it needs to become a mighty oak tree is already inside of it. This is the same with you. Everything you need to be a great athlete is already inside you. Largely in sports, the right conditions have to do with the six inches between your ears—your mind. Are you working out your mind? If you do the right things and create the right conditions, you are likely to become a mighty oak. An acorn thrives in the right conditions: sun, water, soil, and space to grow. But it must avoid negative conditions, too: overcrowding, drought, and squirrels. In your own life right now, what positive conditions are necessary for you to thrive? What are some of the negative conditions—the squirrels—you must avoid?

An acorn in the right conditions will become a mighty oak that can produce in its lifetime millions and millions of acorns. Its life will have a ripple effect. It's the same for you. The potential to be a great athlete is already inside you. If you create the right mental conditions to make this happen, you, too, can thrive. The ripple effect of your performance and of your character can be profound for your team, for your school, for your family, and beyond.

You already have all you need to succeed inside of you. With a clearer preconscious mind, you can begin to compete using all of your mind. Know that when you begin taking care of the six inches between your ears, you will be amazed at what you can do academically, athletically, and beyond, and how well you can do it!

Keegan Longueira's Story

On March 2, 2015 Keegan Longueira of South Africa became the Guinness World Record Holder for the fastest man to ever cross the continent of Africa on bicycle. He rode from

Cairo to Cape Town in fifty-nine days, eight hours, and thirty minutes.

The journey tested his ability to keep his preconscious mind clearer throughout the entire feat. Due to injuries and skin infections, by the time he reached Sudan, he was already four days behind the record pace. Keegan's struggles only continued as he battled diarrhea, severe sunburn, dehydration, and cramps. Twice he even survived near robberies at knifepoint. In Ethiopia, he was spat on and hit with rocks thrown by kids. Yet he pressed on and crossed Sudan, Ethiopia, Kenya, Tanzania, Zambia, and Botswana before eventually arriving back in South Africa.

Before beginning his adventure, Keegan reached out to me. His message follows:

Keegan Longueira
View Profile

Hi there! Im a massive fan of your work!
i WOULD LOVE TO WORK WITH YOU GUYS! I am leaving on an expedition on bicycle to attempt to become the fastest man on bicycle from Cairo to Cape Town.

Would you be intrested in following my trip, giving advice, studying me, looking at why I succeed and why i fail. Im an big follower and watch your youtube videos all the time!

Throughout his journey, Keegan applied the concept of clearer mind, better performance. He embodied the Mind of the Athlete concepts. I actively connected with Keegan to help him raise his awareness, process, commune, integrate, and of course, perform. Keegan was gracious, tenacious, and committed to the sports psychology he received. To his credit, with a clearer mind, he accomplished something no one else in the world has ever done.

Action Steps:

1. Make a list of the positive attributes of your character the world sees when your preconscious mind is

clearer and your performance is better.

2.   Reflect back on a memory when you excelled beyond what you thought was possible. Pay attention to the mental aspects of this great performance and try to replicate them.

3.   Write down the conditions needed for you to thrive.

4.   Identify some upcoming athletic events where you want to perform at your best. Begin to take the steps now to be sure that your preconscious mind is clearer at the time when it matters most.

5.   Be sure to compliment a teammate who is experiencing a clearer mind and better performance.

Summary

There is an effective five-step process for clearing out your preconscious mind. The first step is to be more aware of what is in there. As an athlete, you are so busy that you typically don't have the time to stop and really think about all the experiences in there. In counseling, I'll often ask a person how she is really doing. This is an invitation for her to tell me about what's really going on in her life, what's really in her preconscious mind. We then move onto step 2, which is to process this content. Processing really means talking or writing about it. As we talk about the issues in our preconscious mind, we tend to feel better because we are emotionally resolving those tensions. It is catharsis, which means a freeing of emotions. Step 3 is communing, or connecting with something larger than yourself: a higher power, a greater authority. While communing can take the form of meditation, visualization, or imagery, it is most commonly referred to as prayer. When people take the issues they are struggling with and commune, they often feel better. Step 4 is to integrate, or resolve those "dots" that cloud your preconscious mind. Integrating is the art and science of good counseling, coaching, parenting, or teaching. In essence, it helps people reframe their life experiences from another perspective, which emotionally diffuses those situations. By doing so, the content sinks to the exconscious mind. As material shifts to the exconscious mind, it frees up the preconscious mind, thus making it clearer. When the preconscious mind is clearer, athletes typically do better at step 5, which is to perform. All of the good qualities within a person, such as intelligence, patience, humor, creativity, and love, can flow more easily. As shown in the next diagram, when the preconscious mind is clearer, it clears the path for these positive attributes to rise to the surface of your mind.

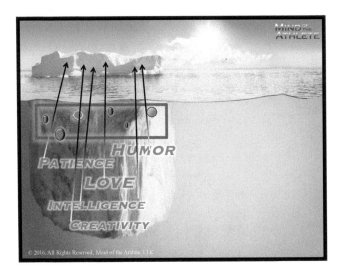

PART 3:
KEY POINTS TO REMEMBER

1. Spending some time alone can help you become *aware* of the thoughts and negative emotions (such as anger, anxiety, hatred) that are flooding your preconscious mind.

2. It's important to *process* the material that is in your preconscious mind. Too much is going on for you to resolve conflicts on your own simply by thinking about them. You can process this information by talking to someone you trust or by journaling—writing it down in a journal or typing it into your phone, computer or tablet.

3. Another strategy that can help you clear your preconscious mind effectively is *communing*—connecting with something larger than yourself: a higher power, a greater authority. Communing is accomplished by linking something in your mind that seems like a big deal to you with the bigger picture, therefore putting it in its proper perspective. Self-reflection, meditation, and prayer are all forms of communing.

4. *Integrating* is the art of positive thinking. It is the art of using thoughts that concern you in a positive way, and it's another important step in clearing your preconscious mind. Integrating allows you to see your thoughts from another angle. Sometimes a coach or someone else you trust can help you see what you thought was a

negative aspect of your performance in a more positive way.

5. Surrounding yourself with positive, trustworthy people makes it easier to integrate your thoughts and keep a positive perspective.

6. Combining all of these strategies can help you clear your preconscious mind and perform at your optimum level.

CONCLUSION

Clearer mind, *better* performance. It's a simple phrase with profoundly potential benefits. You have so much more potential within you than you realize. Unlock it by keeping your preconscious mind clearer. Not only will you feel better, but you will also have a competitive advantage over your opponents.

The path to keeping your preconscious mind clearer is simple. First and foremost, remember the model for how the mind works best. Be sure to recall the three levels of the subconscious mind (preconscious, exconscious, and unconscious) and how they function. Know that the key to high performance is keeping the preconscious mind less cluttered with emotionally charged life experiences.

The preconscious mind is the place in your mind where memories are stored that can easily be recalled but are outside of your immediate awareness. Unfortunately, despite your efforts, at times you will become overextended and emotionally overwhelmed. When this occurs the preconscious mind becomes flooded. Stress ensues. Performance can drop. Many athletes get tripped up by the 5 hurdles of a flooded preconscious mind. Because you now know about these hurdles: insomnia, anxiety, low emotional energy, misguided tensions, and depression, it is less likely you will get tripped up by them. If you do, apply the skills you learned in this book and be sure to get back up on your feet again.

Keep practicing the 5 steps to clearing out your preconscious mind. Take time each day to become more aware of the stressors that are bothering you. Process those stressors with a family member, friend, or counselor. Commune about your stressors. Be wise in discerning whose counsel you accept in resolving emotionally charged experiences in your life; integrating those resolved experiences into your exconscious mind is an important step in clearing your mind. Then, get out there and perform. Let the world see all of your giftedness.

You spend a lot of time, effort, and energy working out your physical body to prepare for competition and excel in your sport. Elevate your training by working out your mind constantly like you work out your body. Keep your mind clearer. You will improve your emotional health. Your performance will get better.

MIND OF THE ATHLETE TRAINING

Congrats on completing the beginning step in your mental training! You now know how the mind works. Now, it is time for you to begin learning many more psychological skills to take your mental training to the next level.

At Mind of the Athlete, it is our passion to educate and equip you with the mental tools you need to thrive. We have a number of options for you to start this training.

Let's begin by having you get connected with our signature mental training offering, which is the Mind of the Athlete Program. This is a 10+ hour video, audio, and worksheet sports psychology curriculum, which is all contained on a single flash drive. This program contains 16 videos on such topics as Sleep, Confidence, Motivation, Psychology of Injury, and Positive Thinking. Each video has an accompanying worksheet. These worksheets contain individual reflection and team conversation topics. The 10 CDs include topics such as Mind of the Parent, Mind of the Coach, and The 5 Hurdles That Trip Up Athletes. You can purchase the program from our online store at mindoftheathlete.com/store.

Also available for purchase on our online store are Mind of the Athlete t-shirts, wristbands with the *Clearer* Mind, *Better* Performance message on them, and Mind of the Athlete journals. Athletes across the country wear the wristbands as a daily reminder to them to take care of their mental health. We also encourage every athlete to write down their thoughts into our journals, as well as the wisdom they are receiving from their coaches each day.

For more selective sports psychology content, you might consider specific Mind of the Athlete CDs. These CDs include Performance Anxiety Management, Visualization for Positive Thinking and Relaxation, Mental Strength, and more. The CDs are available for purchase on our online Mind of the Athlete store (mindoftheathlete.com/store).

Be sure to get connected with our extensive free online resources. Each day on Twitter (@mindofathlete) and Facebook (MindOfTheAthlete) we are posting great content such as research on neuroscience, pop culture references to athletes benefitting from sports psychology, and our own sports psychology videos. In fact, there are over 500 of our own videos on the Mind of the Athlete YouTube page (youtube.com/mindoftheathlete.com). We continually create and post videos weekly to provide you with cutting edge content. Regarding inspiration, you will find a wealth of it on our Instagram page (mindoftheathlete), which contains over 600 photos with original quotes from our staff. Many teams have these inspirational photos hanging in their locker rooms.

If you are not yet receiving it, we highly encourage you to sign up to receive the weekly Mind of the Athlete blog. These concise and powerful blogs will provide you with a nugget of sports psychology content that is grounded, relevant, and applicable. Thousands of people read them each week. You also have access to over 150 of these blogs at mindoftheathlete.com/site/blog. Sign up to receive these blogs at our website www.mindoftheathlete.com.

The best way for you to develop even more skills to have a clearer mind and better performance is to start working one-on-one with a Mind of the Athlete team member.

We would be happy to speak with you about beginning a one-on-one coaching program that is customized to your specific needs, level, and goals. You can learn more about this offering via our website www.mindoftheathlete.com.

Consider bringing us to your school for keynote speaking. We offer a number of speeches, such as *Mind of the Athlete: Clearer Mind, Better Performance, Sleep: The Number One Factor in Performance, Performance Anxiety: Less Nervousness, More Excitement,* and *The Five Hurdles: How Athletes Often Fall and Can Rise Again.* Please call for pricing and availability. In addition to our keynote speeches, we can also come to your school to provide team consulting.

If your team or school is really passionate about getting sports psychology content to its athletes, please contact us regarding speaking at your school. As frequent speakers and consultants in schools across the country, we have a wide variety of topics you can select.

We can help you work on your mind as hard as you have been working on your body. We are excited for you to get more connected with Mind of the Athlete so that you can develop even more skills in order to have a clearer mind and better performance.

ABOUT THE AUTHOR

Jarrod Spencer, Psy.D.
President and Founder
Mind of the Athlete, LLC

3400 Bath Pike, Ste. 302
Bethlehem, PA 18017
610.867.7770
drjarrod@mindoftheathlete.com
www.mindoftheathlete.com

Jarrod Spencer is a sports psychologist whose passion is to help athletes attain peak performance through sound emotional health. He is a trusted, leading authority on the mind of today's athlete and is driven to educate others regarding how the mind works best.

Dr. Spencer's teachings focus on the idea that a clearer mind leads to better performance. Influenced by views in neuroscience, psychoanalysis, Christianity, and peak-performance literature, Dr. Spencer has a heart to serve athletes by improving their overall well-being while nurturing their emotional health.

Dr. Spencer's communication style is positive, proactive, and results-oriented. His highly successful approach is a direct result of his warmth, insight, and dynamic teaching style. Desiring to take athletes one step further than they have gone before, Dr. Spencer uses a blend of the "outside in" and "inside out" learning methods to help athletes become unstuck and reach their true potential. It is this combination of learning modalities that allows athletes to excel faster and go deeper with long-lasting positive mental results.

Dr. Spencer is president and founder of Mind of the Athlete, LLC, a sports psychology company committed to improving the emotional health of athletes. He is the creator of the Mind of the Athlete Program, a cutting-edge video and audio sports psychology curriculum. This program, made up of sixteen videos, sixteen accompanying worksheets, and ten CDs, is currently used worldwide in countries such as South Africa, Ireland, and South Korea. He is also co-author of *The Sky Is Not the Limit: Discovering the True North for Your Life's Path*.

Dr. Spencer works with professional, Olympic, college, and high school athletes, coaches, and teams across the country. In addition to serving as the sports psychologist for athletic teams at such schools as the University of Maryland, Old Dominion University, Lehigh University, and Lafayette College, Dr. Spencer also works individually with athletes from the University of Michigan, the University of North Carolina, The Ohio State University, Princeton University, and many more.

He is a fixture in media. Dr. Spencer has been featured in the *USA Today* and New York Daily News newspapers. Currently, Dr. Spencer serves as a frequent guest on WFMZ Morning News and has been featured on "The Peak" TV show. Dr. Spencer has been heard on ESPN Radio of the Lehigh Valley, highlighting and explaining the psychology of current events in sports. He also starred in the TV Show "What the Heck Were They Thinking?!" with former heavyweight boxing champion Larry Holmes. Additionally, Dr. Spencer created and starred on the TV show "Mind of the Athlete."

Dr. Spencer has extensive training and experience in the field of health and sports psychology. Before earning a Doctor of Psychology degree from The Illinois School of Professional Psychology in Chicago, he earned his master's degree in clinical psychology from West Chester University and his bachelor's degree in psychobiology from Lafayette College. He trained professionally at The Jersey Shore Medical Center, Northwestern Neuropsychological Association, and The Diamond Headache Clinic. He is a licensed psychologist in Pennsylvania, Maryland, and Virginia. Dr. Spencer is also a member of The American Psychological Association, Pennsylvania Psychological Association, and Lehigh Valley Psychological and Counseling Association.

As an athlete, Dr. Spencer was an All-State high school wrestler who captained his team to back-to-back New Jersey state championships. While in college, he was a tailback for the Lafayette College football team. Also, while attending graduate school at West Chester University, he played wing on the rugby team.

Dr. Spencer resides in the beautiful Lehigh Valley of Pennsylvania with his wife and three children.

ENDNOTES

1. Justin Ching, "Mental Health Issues a Challenge for NCAA in Regard to Student-Athletes," March 25, 2015, FOX Sports website, http://www.foxsports.com/other/story/madison-holleran-ncaa-student-athletes-mental-health-issues-032515.

2. "Spring 2013 Reference Group Executive Summary," National College Health Assessment, American College Health Association website, http://www.acha-ncha.org/docs/ACHA-NCHA-II_ReferenceGroup_ExecutiveSUmmary_Spring2013.pdf.

3. "Fall 2015 Reference Group Executive Summary," National College Health Assessment, American College Health Association website, http://www.acha-ncha.org/docs/NCHA-IIFALL2015REFERENCE GROUPEXECUTIVE20SUMMARY.pdf.

4. Ann Kearns Davoren and Seunghyun Hwang, "Mind, Body, and Sport: Depression and Anxiety Prevalence in Student-Athletes," October 8, 2014, National Collegiate Athletic Association (NCAA) website, http://www.ncaa.org/health-and-safety/sport-science-institute/mind-body-and-sport-depression-and-anxiety-prevalence-student-athletes.

5. Michael Grandner, "Mind, Body, and Sport: Sleeping Disorders," NCAA website, http://www.ncaa.org/health-and-safety/sport-science-institute/mind-body-and-sport-sleeping-disorders.

6. "Journal of Behavioral Addictions," August 24, 2014, NCBI website, http://www.ncbi.nlm.nih.gov/pmc/articles/PMC4291831/.

7. "Suicide Trends among Persons Aged 10–24 Years—United States, 1994–2012," Morbidity and Mortality Weekly Report, March 6, 2015, Centers for Disease Control and Prevention website, http://www.cdc.gov/mmwr/preview/mmwrhtml/mm6408a1.htm.

8. National Association of Anorexia Nervosa and Associated Disorders

(ANAD), http://www.anad.org/get-information/about-eating-disorders/eating-disorders-statistics/.

9. Jeff Hawkins, "Allison Schmitt Opens Up about Post-Olympic Depression," May 20, 2015, Team USA website, http://m.teamusa.org/News/2015/May/20/Allison-Schmitt-Makes-A-Difference-In-And-Out-Of-The-Pool.

10. Lisa La Rose, "Beyond Bullying: The Long-Term Effects of Hazing on Young Adults," October 20, 2014, Theravive website, http://www.theravive.com/blog/post/2014/10/20/Beyond-Bullying-The-Long-Term-Effects-of-Hazing-on-Young-Adults.aspx.

11. Ibid.

12. Ibid.

13. "Substance Abuse," Office of Adolescent Health website, http://www.hhs.gov/ash/oah/adolescent-health-topics/substance-abuse/home.html.

14. "Fact Sheets: Underage Drinking," Centers for Disease Control and Prevention website, http://www.cdc.gov/alcohol/fact-sheets/underage-drinking.htm.http://www.cdc.gov/mmwr/preview/mmwrhtml/ss6304a1.htm?s_cid=ss6304a1_e.

15. L. Jon Wertheim and Ken Rodriguez, "Smack Epidemic: How Painkillers Are Turning Athletes into Heroin Addicts at an Alarming Rate," Sports Illustrated website, June 18, 2015, http://www.si.com/more-sports/2015/06/18/special-report-painkillers-young-athletes-heroin-addicts.

16. Brendan Duffy, "Sleep and Athletic Performance: Winning the Game with Quality Sleep," April 21, 2015, American Association of Sleep Technologists blog, http://blog.aastweb.org/sleep-and-athletic-performance-winning-the-game-with-quality-sleep.

17. *Medical News Today*, "Anxiety: Causes, Symptoms, and Treatments," August 3, 2015, http://www.medicalnewstoday.com/info/anxiety.

18. Mayo Clinic, "Panic Attacks and Panic Disorder," May 19, 2015,

http://www.mayoclinic.org/diseases-conditions/panic-attacks/basics/definition/con-20020825.

19. "Vital Signs," Cleveland Clinic website, http://my.clevelandclinic.org/health/healthy_living/hic_Pre-participation_Evaluations/hic_Vital_Signs.

20. "Probability of Competing in Sports Beyond High School," National Collegiate Athletic Association (NCAA) website, http://www.ncaa.org/about/resources/research/probability-competing-beyond-high-school.

21. "Fall 2016 Reference Group Executive Summary," National College Health Assessment, American College Health Association, http://www.acha-ncha.org/docs/NCHA-II_FALL_2016_REFERENCE_GROUP_EXECUTIVE_SUMMARY.pdf.

22. Ibid.

23. Susan Krauss Whitbourne, PhD, "How Casual Sex Can Affect Our Mental Health," March 9, 2013, Psychology Today blog, https://www.psychologytoday.com/blog/fulfillment-any-age/201303/how-casual-sex-can-affect-our-mental-health.

24. NAMI, "Mental Illness Prolific Among College Students," August 2004, http://www.nami.org/Press-Media/Press-Releases/2004/Mental-Illness-Prolific-Among-College-Students.

25. Marin Cogan, "The pursuit of 'radical acceptance'," June 25, 2014, ESPN website, http://www.espn.com/nfl/story/_/page/hotread140707/chicago-bears-brandon-marshall-spreads-awareness-nfl-mental-health-crisis-espn-magazine. Project 375 website, https://project375.org/.

26. Joe Lapointe, The New York Times, "Counseling is Helping Rodriquez Face Heat," May 2005, http://www.nytimes.com/2005/05/26/sports/baseball/counseling-is-helping-rodriguez-face-heat.html?_r=0.

27. Anthony "A. B." Bourke, "The Five R's of an Effective Debrief: Part Three of Three," Successful Meetings website, February 4, 2014,

http://www.successfulmeetings.com/strategy/meeting-strategies/the-five-rs-of-an-effective-debrief--part-three-of-three/.

28. Gary Mihoces, "New Guidelines Established for Young Athletes Who Face Mental Health Issues," March 2, 2015, USA Today website, http://usatodayhss.com/2015/nata-tim-neal-mental-health-issues-in-student-athletes.

29. Nick Firchau, "Landon Donovan's Other Legacy: Challenging the Stigma of Mental Health," January 4, 2015, MLS Soccer website, http://www.mlssoccer.com/news/article/2014/11/20/landon-donovans-other-legacy-challenging-stigma-mental-health-word.

30. "Spirituality, Religion May Protect against Major Depression by Thickening Brain Cortex," January 16, 2014, Science Daily website, http://www.sciencedaily.com/releases/2014/01/140116084846.htm.

31. Gary Scott Smith, "Americans Are Deeply Religious, So Will We Ever See an Athiest President? Here's What We Know," March 23, 2015, The Washington Post website, http://www.washingtonpost.com/news/acts-of-faith/wp/2015/03/23/americans-are-deeply-religious-so-will-we-ever-see-an-atheist-president-heres-what-we-know/.

32. Anita Manning, "Prayer Effective as Painkiller?" May 9, 2005, USA Today website, http://usatoday30.usatoday.com/news/health/2005-05-09-prayer-pain_x.htm.

33. "Healing and the Role of Prayer," December 23, 2013, Canyon Ranch website, http://www.canyonranch.com/your-health/mind-spirit/cultivating-happiness/your-spiritual-path/healing-and-the-role-prayer.

34. Alan Lew, This Is Real and You Are Completely Unprepared: The Days of Awe as a Journey of Transformation (New York: Little, Brown and Company), 69.

35. Vanessa Garcia Rodriguez, "Faith Drives Golden State Warriors Point Guard Stephen Curry," May 22, 2015, Christian Examiner website,

http://www.christianexaminer.com/article/faith.drives.golden.state.warriors.point.guard.stephen.curry/48981.htm.

36. "Changing the Game in Youth Sports: John O'Sullivan at TEDxBend," YouTube, https://www.youtube.com/watch?v=VXw0XGOVQvw.

37. "Tiger Woods Exclusive Interview from ESPN SportsCenter," YouTube video, March 21, 2010, https://www.youtube.com/watch?v=X7T8I_Sjads.

CPSIA information can be obtained
at www.ICGtesting.com
Printed in the USA
BVHW05s1530080918
526882BV00005B/7/P

9 780996 964999